THE BIBLE STORY

VOLUME IV

Heroes and Heroines

The BIBLE STORY

More Than Four Hundred Stories in Ten Volumes
Covering the Entire Bible From Genesis to Revelation

VOLUME FOUR
Heroes and Heroines

BY ARTHUR S. MAXWELL

Author of *Uncle Arthur's Bedtime Stories, The Children's Hour With Uncle Arthur,*
The Secret of the Cave, etc.

•

REVIEW AND HERALD PUBLISHING ASSOCIATION
Washington, D.C.

CONTENTS

5

← PAINTING BY RUSSELL HARLAN   © 1955, BY REVIEW AND HERALD

Saul honored David for slaying Goliath
by putting him over all his fighting men.
Jonathan, the king's son, gave him royal
garments, and they became lifelong friends.

PART I

Stories of David
(1 Samuel 16:14-31:13)

The Lord is my shepherd; I shall not want. ✦ He maketh me to lie down in green pastures: he leadeth me beside the still waters. ✦ He restoreth my soul: he leadeth me in the paths of righteousness for his name's sake. ✦ Yea, though I walk through the valley of the shadow of death, I will fear no evil: for thou art with me; thy rod and thy staff they comfort me. ✦ Thou preparest a table before me in the presence of mine enemies: thou anointest my head with oil; my cup runneth over. ✦ Surely goodness and mercy shall follow me all the days of my life: and I will dwell in the house of the Lord for ever. ⋯ Psalm 23.

STORY 1

David the Lionhearted

I T WAS lonesome about the house. Three of David's older brothers had gone to help Saul fight the Philistines. Father and Mother were worrying about what might happen to them on the battlefield.

David was worried too. Out there on the hillside, looking after the sheep, he kept thinking about Eliab, Abinadab, and Shammah. Perhaps they would be killed or taken prisoners, and he would never see them again. That made him sad.

As he lay on the soft green grass, with the sheep feeding around him and the cool wind blowing over him, he wondered why people had to fight and kill each other. Then he remembered how one day a lion had come to attack his sheep, and he had fought and killed it all by himself. Would he ever forget that lion—or the bear that had tried to make off with one of his lambs? He hadn't wanted to kill them, but there was no other way to protect the sheep.

But the Philistines were different. They should have known

9

As a shepherd boy, David faithfully tended his father's sheep. Alone with his flocks in the fields he learned lessons of God's love, and later wrote the beautiful shepherd psalm.

better. Why didn't they stay in their own country? Why did they have to come and bother other people as they did?

Suddenly from far away came a familiar call.

"David!"

It was Jesse, his father. He wanted to send some food to the boys in camp. Would David please take it? Would he! There was nothing he wanted to do more. Perhaps he would be there in time to see the battle. Maybe he would get a good look at the Philistines and find out what sort of people they were.

"And David rose up early in the morning, and left the sheep with a keeper, and took, and went, as Jesse had commanded him."

How far he had to travel we are not told, but at last he came to the camp. Here he left the food with the man in charge, then ran among the soldiers until he found his brothers.

How glad he was to see them again! But Eliab, the eldest, did not give him a very happy greeting. He asked, angrily, why he had come and with whom he had left the sheep. "I know thy pride," he said, "and the naughtiness of thine heart; for thou art come down that thou mightest see the battle."

"What have I now done?" sighed David, like any boy who has been rebuked by an elder brother.

Just then someone shouted, "Look, there he comes!"

David looked and, to his amazement, out of the camp of the Philistines came a giant of a man, at least nine feet tall, wearing a huge brass helmet, a brass coat of mail, and brass armor on his legs. As for the staff of his spear, it was "like a weaver's beam; and his spear's head weighed six hundred shekels of iron: and one bearing a shield went before him."

"Who's that?" asked David.

"Goliath of Gath," said someone, beginning to run away as the giant strode down into the valley which separated the two armies.

Why is everybody running away? wondered David. Why doesn't somebody stand up to this man, giant though he is?

Disappointed and angry, he said aloud, "Who is this uncircumcised Philistine, that he should defy the armies of the living God?"

Somebody heard what he said and told King Saul, who sent for David.

"Let no man's heart fail because of him," David said to the king. "Thy servant will go and fight with this Philistine."

Saul wouldn't hear of it. "You can't go," he said in effect, "you're too young."

But David told the king about his fight with the lion and the bear, adding, "The Lord that delivered me out of the paw of the lion, and out of the paw of the bear, he will deliver me out of the hand of this Philistine."

At last King Saul was convinced. He saw here a boy with the heart of a lion and strong in the strength of

God. He told David he could go and fight Goliath if he wanted to, and gave him a suit of his own armor to protect him.

Of course, the armor was too big. Nothing fitted. David felt uncomfortable. "I cannot go with these," he said, and took the armor all off again.

Then, staff in his hand, he walked down to the brook in the valley and carefully chose five smooth stones, putting them in the shepherd's bag which he carried.

What in the world is he doing? everybody wondered, as they watched him calmly picking up one stone after another and judging them for weight and shape and smoothness. Is he just going to throw stones at the man?

They wondered even more as they saw him walk toward the towering figure of the waiting Philistine with no weapon but a sling.

As David drew nearer, Goliath became very angry, and cursed him by his gods.

"Am I a dog," he cried, "that thou comest to me with staves? Come to me, and I will give thy flesh unto the fowls of the air, and to the beasts of the field."

David took no notice. Instead, without a trace of fear, he replied, in never-to-be-forgotten words: "Thou comest to me with a sword, and with a spear, and with a shield: but I come to thee in the name of the Lord of hosts, the God of the armies of Israel, whom thou hast defied.

"This day will the Lord deliver thee into mine hand . . . ; that all the earth may know that there is a God in Israel. And all this assembly shall know that the Lord saveth not with

12

sword and spear: for the battle is the Lord's, and he will give you into our hands."

This was too much for Goliath. His face livid with anger, he lunged forward, his enormous spear grasped tightly in his massive hands.

Still David did not flinch. Instead, he calmly took one of the stones from his bag, put it in his sling, and threw it with all his strength at the advancing giant.

The watching thousands held their breath. Everyone knew there could be no second shot.

Suddenly Goliath stopped, stumbled, fell, his huge spear clattering to the ground. The pebble had struck him in the forehead, the one unprotected place on his body.

Running toward the fallen Philistine, David drew the giant's sword and cut off his head.

The battle was as good as over. Seeing their champion dead, the rest of the Philistines fled in terror, the Israelites chasing them clear back to their own country.

How much God can do through one dear boy who loves and trusts Him with all his heart!

STORY 2

Winning a Princess

THE DAY David slew Goliath was a turning point in his life. He never went back to his sheep.

"Saul took him that day, and would let him go no more home to his father's house."

For a while he was everybody's hero. King and people loved him dearly.

Jonathan, Saul's son, took a great fancy to the young shepherd boy, giving him "his garments, even to his sword, and to his bow." This meant a lot in those days.

Young as he was, David was set "over the men of war, and he was accepted in the sight of all the people, and also in the sight of Saul's servants."

Some boys' heads would have been turned by so much praise, but not David's. He "behaved himself wisely in all his ways; and the Lord was with him."

Once when he returned from another successful attack upon the Philistines, "the women came out of all cities of Israel, singing and dancing, to meet king Saul, with tabrets, with joy, and with instruments of musick. And the women answered one another as they played, and said, Saul hath slain his thousands, and David his ten thousands."

This was too much for Saul. He began to feel jealous of David. He didn't like having the people say that David was ten times as good a soldier as he. The Bible says, "Saul eyed David from that day forward."

Next day, brooding on what the women had sung, he suddenly became so angry that he threw a javelin at David as he was playing a musical instrument in the palace. Fortunately David saw the weapon coming, and dodged out of its way.

Even so the king did not forget his promise to give his daughter in marriage to the man who killed Goliath. He

couldn't. Too many people had heard him say he would do so, and, knowing how much they loved David, he did not dare go back on his word.

Still, he cheated. And "it came to pass at the time when Merab Saul's daughter should have been given to David, that she was given unto Adriel."

Then he sent word to David that he could marry his other daughter, Michal, if he would go and kill a hundred Philistines. He hoped that David would be killed in the fighting, but he wasn't. He came back alive and victorious. And now there was nothing Saul could do but give him Michal.

So the shepherd boy won a princess and became the king's son-in-law.

I wish I could say that they lived happily ever after, but they didn't. True, "Michal Saul's daughter loved him," but, alas, "Saul was yet the more afraid of David," and became his enemy "continually."

It could have been such a happy family if only envy and jealousy hadn't spoiled it all.

STORY 3

Dummy in Bed

NOW THAT David was married to Michal, you would think that King Saul would have got over all his unkind feelings toward the young man. Not so. Instead, he became more and more angry with him, and even told his son Jonathan to kill him.

That was the last thing Jonathan intended to do. He loved David, and warned him of his danger. Then he went to his father and pleaded with him to spare David's life. He reminded Saul of how David had slain Goliath. "You were there," he said; "you saw it happen, and you were happy about it; then why 'slay David without a cause?' " he asked.

Jonathan won. Saul said he wouldn't kill David after all.

Very happy, Jonathan ran to where David was hiding, and told him he could come back to the court and everything would be all right. So David returned and was given his old job in the army again.

For a while everything was peaceful, and David played

music for the king as he had often done many times before.

Then war broke out again with the Philistines, and David was sent to fight them. Once more he returned victorious, and once more, of course, everybody cheered him. Everybody, that is, except Saul. His old jealousy returned. He couldn't stand having the people say so many nice things about David. In a fit of rage he threw his javelin at him again.

Fortunately the weapon missed him and stuck in the palace wall, but David thought it was time to go. Slipping out of the room, he hurried home and told Michal what had happened.

She was worried now. This time, she felt sure, her father would not change his mind. David would have to run away at once and hide. "If thou save not thy life to night," she said, "to morrow thou shalt be slain."

Even while they talked together there was a banging at the door of their house. David guessed it was Saul's soldiers, come to take him prisoner, maybe to kill him. What should he do? He could go to the door and fight them, but that might start a rebellion against the king, and he didn't want to do that. He could meekly surrender, or he could run away.

He made up his mind. He would leave. But how?

"The window," suggested Michal.

They opened it. The night was dark. David climbed out and let himself down to the ground. There was a whispered good-by and he was gone.

Michal closed the window and quickly put an image in David's bed to make it look as if he were in it, fast asleep. Then she answered the door.

18

"He's sick," she said sadly to the king's messengers. "He's in bed asleep; don't wake him up."

They demanded to see for themselves, so she let them in. There was but little light in the room. They took one look at the figure in the bed and concluded that if David was lying as still as that he must be very ill indeed. Then they went and told the king.

Saul was furious. He ordered them to go and fetch David, bed and all. "Bring him up to me in the bed," he cried, "that I may slay him."

The messengers obeyed. But when they went to pick up the bed, they soon saw how they had been tricked, for "behold, there was an image in the bed, with a pillow of goats' hair for his bolster."

What they said when they saw that dummy, we are not told. Maybe some of them laughed. But Saul didn't. He sent for Michal and gave her a real talking to for deceiving him.

She didn't mind. She knew her father wouldn't kill her. And meanwhile David was safe, hurrying as fast as he could to Ramah to tell Samuel all that had happened.

19

STORY 4

A Tale of Three Arrows

DAVID might have fled to his home in Bethlehem and talked to his father and mother. But he didn't. He wanted to see the man of God who had anointed him. Life had become such a muddle. He had tried so hard to do right, and now all this trouble had come to him. He wondered why, and what he should do next.

"So David fled, and escaped, and came to Samuel to Ramah, and told him all that Saul had done to him."

It was a long story David had to tell, and Samuel must have been very disappointed at the way the king had treated this fine young man who had done so much for Israel.

Just what Samuel said to David we do not know, but we can be sure he told him to be patient and to trust God to work everything out right in the end.

Not long after this David met Jonathan again. They were so glad to see each other and David said, "What have I done? what is mine iniquity? and what is my sin before thy father, that he seeketh my life?" He couldn't understand why Saul would want to kill his own son-in-law.

Jonathan told him not to worry; he would let David know in good time if there was any real danger.

But David was greatly troubled. "Truly as the Lord liveth," he said, "there is but a step between me and death."

Then he told what was worrying him now. It would soon be time for the feast of the new moon, when the king expected everybody to be present. Maybe Saul would miss him and maybe he wouldn't. Yet he didn't dare go, not as things were now. So he asked Jonathan to let him know what happened.

Jonathan promised to do so, "because he loved him: for he loved him as he loved his own soul."

Then they made a plan. David was to hide in a certain place near a field they both knew well. Then, after the feast, Jonathan would come to the field, shoot three arrows, and say to his arrow boy, "Go, find out the arrows." If he called to the boy, "The arrows are on this side of thee," then David would know that all was well, and that the king had got over his fit of rage; but if he called to the boy, "The arrows are beyond thee," then David would know that the king was still angry and he had better stay away.

Well, the feast began, and "David's place was empty." Saul said nothing about it the first day, but on the second day

he turned to Jonathan and asked where David was. "Wherefore cometh not the son of Jesse to meat, neither yesterday, nor to day?" he said.

He might have guessed, if he had stopped to think how badly he had treated David a little while before. But he didn't. So Jonathan made some excuse about David's wanting to go to see his family in Bethlehem.

At once Saul suspected that the two young men had fixed this up together. "Thou perverse rebel!" he yelled at Jonathan in front of everybody, "as long as the son of Jesse liveth upon the ground, thou shalt not be established, nor thy kingdom. Wherefore now send and fetch him unto me, for he shall surely die."

Now Jonathan was angry. "Wherefore shall he be slain?" he cried. "What hath he done?"

Trembling with rage, Saul seized his javelin and threw it at his son. But his aim was bad, and Jonathan left the table "in fierce anger."

22

Early next morning he went to the field
with his arrow boy. Fitting an arrow to his bow, he said
to the lad, "Run, find out now the arrows which I shoot."
And the boy obeyed.

When the lad came to the place where the arrow had
stuck in the ground, Jonathan called aloud, so that David could
hear him, "Is not the arrow beyond thee?" Then again to
the boy, but really to David, he called, "Make speed, haste,
stay not."

The arrow boy picked up the three arrows and returned.
Jonathan then handed him his bow and sent him back to the
city. When the boy was out of sight, David came out of his
hiding place, and Jonathan told him all that had happened.
Then they kissed each other and wept.

"The Lord be between me and thee, and between my
seed and thy seed for ever," said Jonathan as the tears rolled
down their cheeks.

It was a sad parting. Both knew it would be a long time
before they would meet again.

23

STORY 5

Goliath's Sword

THIS time David did not go to Ramah, but to Nob, where lived Ahimelech, the high priest, and his son Abiathar, probably serving jointly with his father.

When Ahimelech saw David he scented trouble. "Why art thou alone?" he asked, for at first he did not see the other young men who had come with him.

David made some excuse about being on a secret mission for the king, but the high priest must have wondered why, if this were true, David should be so hungry. For David's next question was, "What do you have to eat?"

Ahimelech said he didn't have anything except the shew-bread, and, of course, this was holy.

David said that that would be all right; he would take that, if he could have it. "So the priest gave him hallowed bread," five loaves in all.

Long years afterward Jesus told this story to the Jewish leaders of His day. When the Pharisees were finding fault with

24

His disciples for picking ears of corn on the Sabbath, He said
to them, "Have ye never read what David did, when he had
need, and was an hungred, he, and they that were with him?
How he went into the house of God in the days of Abiathar
the high priest, and did eat the shewbread, which is not lawful
to eat but for the priests, and gave also to them which were
with him?" From this Jesus drew the lesson that "the sabbath
was made for man, and not man for the sabbath." Mark 2:25-28.

When David had eaten he made another strange request
of the high priest. Was there a sword or a spear anywhere
about that he could have?

Ahimelech looked at him in amazement. Imagine David
without a sword or a spear! How could this be? David explained that he had come away from the court in such a hurry
he had left his weapons behind, and "the king's business re-
quired haste."

Usually, of course, there were no weapons in the tabernacle,
but, said Ahimelech, it so happened that there was "the sword
of Goliath the Philistine, whom thou slewest in the valley of

25

Elah, behold, it is here wrapped in a cloth behind the ephod: if thou wilt take that, take it."

David was delighted. "There is none like that," he said, "give it me."

Taking the great sword from the priest, he hurried off to the city of Gath and took refuge there.

Sad to say, one of Saul's servants had been in the tabernacle at the same time as David, and had seen and heard everything. "His name was Doeg, an Edomite, the chiefest of the herdmen that belonged to Saul." This man ran as fast as he could to the king and told him how Ahimelech had given David some of the shewbread and the sword of Goliath.

Greatly angered, the king sent for all the priests of Nob and accused them of plotting against him.

Ahimelech was shocked. He did not know that there was any trouble between Saul and David, and told the king so.

26

"And who is so faithful among all thy servants as David," he said, "which is the king's son in law, and goeth at thy bidding, and is honourable in thine house?"

The king wouldn't listen. He was sure Ahimelech was lying to him.

"Thou shalt surely die, Ahimelech," he said sternly, "thou, and all thy father's house."

Without another word he ordered the guard to kill Ahimelech and all the priests that were with him. But the guard refused to obey him. They "would not put forth their hand to fall upon the priests of the Lord."

So the angry king turned to Doeg and told him to do this wicked thing. Being an Edomite, Doeg didn't care that these men were priests of the Lord, so he slew them. Then he went to Nob and killed all their women and children.

Fortunately Abiathar escaped. He fled to where David was in hiding.

You can imagine how David felt when he heard the news. He was terribly sorry. "I knew it," he said, "that day, when Doeg the Edomite was there, that he would surely tell Saul: I have occasioned the death of all the persons of thy father's house."

But, he added, "Abide thou with me, fear not: for he that seeketh my life, seeketh thy life: but with me thou shalt be in safeguard."

So the two young men stayed together, trusting God to watch over them and to work everything out right for them in His own good time.

27

STORY 6

Song in a Cave

FROM now on David lived a very hard life. He had no home any more. He could not go to see his wife, for King Saul would have soon found out; and he dared not stay with his parents in Bethlehem, lest trouble should come to them. So he slept out in the forest or in the caves of the mountains.

One of these caves was called the cave of Adullam, and he stayed there for some time. His brothers came to see him there "and all his father's house." Other people came, too, for "every one that was in distress, and every one that was in debt, and every one that was discontented, gathered themselves unto him; and he became a captain over them."

One by one they came to him, from all parts of the country, until he had a little army of four hundred men.

It was a very rough group, for every one had a grievance of some kind or other, and it would have been easy for them to become a band of thieves and cutthroats, preying upon

28

the countryside. But David let them know that wasn't his purpose. He told them about God, and many times he sang to them of God's glory and love as he had sung years before on the hillside while tending his sheep.

Here it was, in the cave of Adullam, that he wrote that lovely song which later became known as the fifty-seventh psalm. Read it tonight and think of the cave in which it was written, and of the four hundred men gathered round David as he sang to them.

"Be merciful unto me, O God, be merciful unto me: for my soul trusteth in thee: yea, in the shadow of thy wings will

I make my refuge, until these calamities be overpast. . . . He shall send from heaven, and save me from the reproach of him that would swallow me up. . . .

"My heart is fixed, O God, my heart is fixed: I will sing and give praise. Awake up, my glory; awake, psaltery and harp: I myself will awake early.

"I will praise thee, O Lord, among the people: I will sing unto thee among the nations. For thy mercy is great unto the heavens, and thy truth unto the clouds. Be thou exalted, O God, above the heavens: let thy glory be above all the earth."

Try to picture the scene: the dark cave, lit by a few smoky torches; at one end the brave young man who killed Goliath, his rugged new-found friends sitting and lying on the floor about him; in his hand a harp, which he plays as he sings the praises of God. Suddenly the cave becomes a temple, and sad, bitter men, who have lost all hope, feel hope and faith and love surge back into their hearts again.

About this time David did a very beautiful thing. Leaving the cave of Adullam one day, he went to see the king of Moab to ask a special favor.

"Let my father and my mother, I pray thee, come forth, and be with you, till I know what God will do for me."

The king of Moab was friendly, and agreed to the plan. So David went to Bethlehem and took his parents to the land of Moab, and there they stayed "all the while" that David was in trouble.

How kind of him to remember the old folks and take them to a place of safety!

30

STORY 7

A God-led Life

DAVID had a very simple faith. He took all his worries to God. Whenever he did not know what to do, or which way to go, he asked God about it, and God told him.

One day word came to him that the Philistines were attacking the town of Keilah and stealing grain from the people's barns. At once he wanted to go to the rescue of these people, but as he thought it over he realized that to do so would mean leaving the safety of the cave and going out where Saul might catch him.

What should he do? He talked to God about it. "Shall I go and smite these Philistines?" he asked. And God said, "Go, and smite the Philistines, and save Keilah."

When he told his men what he planned to do, some of them thought it wasn't wise. The danger would be too great, they said.

So David talked to God again. This time God said to

him, "Arise, go down to Keilah; for I will deliver the Philistines into thine hand."

So David decided to go and help Keilah. His band now numbered six hundred men, and together they defeated the Philistines, and not only saved the people of Keilah but won back all their cattle.

You can imagine what a wonderful welcome he and his men received when they returned to Keilah after driving off the Philistines. But they did not enjoy it long.

While David and his men were fighting the Philistines, word reached King Saul that they had left their mountain hideout and gone to Keilah.

Saul was sure he would capture David now, "for," he said, "he is shut in, by entering into a town that hath gates and bars." So he called upon Israel to go down to Keilah to besiege David and his men.

He forgot one important thing—that David was doing his best to walk with God and live a God-led life.

Somehow David learned what Saul was planning to do. Though there was no radio, television, or telephone in those days, the news got through to him. And when he heard it he turned to God and asked, "Will Saul come down . . . ? O Lord God of Israel, I beseech thee, tell thy servant."

God answered, "He will come down."

Then David wanted to know whether he should stay or flee. If the people of Keilah would stand by him, and help him, he thought he might be able to win the battle. If not, he would be in very great danger.

32

A GOD-LED LIFE

So he asked God, "Will the men of Keilah deliver me and my men into the hand of Saul?"

Back came the answer, "They will deliver thee up."

So again David knew what to do. With his six hundred men he left town at once for the safety of the wilderness.

It is good to be able to talk to God like that. And God is as willing to talk to boys and girls today as He was to talk with David in the long ago. He will lead us all the way.

STORY 8

A Very Close Shave

AFTER David and his men left Keilah it seems that they couldn't get back to the cave of Adullam, so they went and lived in a wood on a mountainside in the wilderness of Ziph.

Here David had a visitor whom he had not seen for a long time. It was his old friend Jonathan. Somehow the young prince had found out where he was, and had taken the risk of coming to see him. How glad the two friends must have been to see each other again! And what a lot of things they had to talk about!

Jonathan was sorry for all the trouble that had come to David, but "fear not," he said to him, "for the hand of Saul my father shall not find thee; and thou shalt be king over Israel, and I shall be next unto thee; and that also my father knoweth."

It was clear now what was the matter with Saul. He was afraid that David might become king someday, so he wanted

34

to kill him and get him out of the way. But Jonathan was sure God was with David and that one day the kingdom would be his. How noble it was of him, the king's own son, and heir to the throne, to say, "I will be next unto thee"! It takes much meekness and grace to say that.

At last the two young friends had to say good-by, "and David abode in the wood, and Jonathan went to his house." Probably he went by night, for you can imagine what the king would have said if he had learned where his son had been.

But though Jonathan was so friendly, the natives of the wilderness were not.

Some of them, thinking to gain favor with the king, went and told him exactly where David and his men were living. Worse still, they offered to lead Saul's soldiers to the very spot. "Our part," they said, "shall be to deliver him into the king's hand."

Saul was pleased, but he wanted to make quite sure.

"Go, I pray you," he said to these Ziphites, "prepare yet, and know and see his place where his haunt is, and who hath seen him there: for it is told me that he dealeth very subtilly. See therefore, and take knowledge of all the lurking places

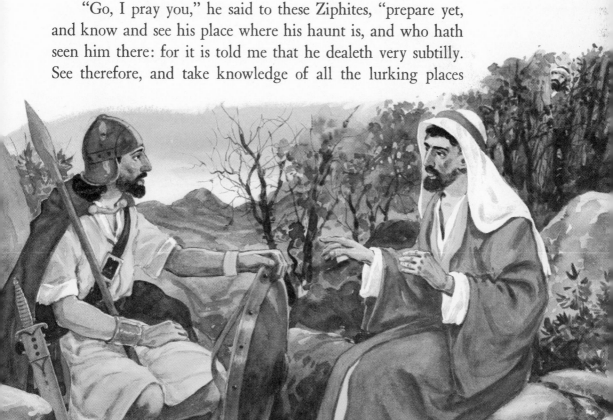

where he hideth himself, and come ye again to me with the certainty, and I will go with you: and it shall come to pass, that if he be in the land, that I will search him out throughout all the thousands of Judah."

This time Saul thought he really would catch David. The spies were so certain they knew exactly where he was hiding. Being dwellers in the wilderness, they claimed to know all David's "lurking places." But smart as they were, they weren't quite as smart as David. For when they led Saul's soldiers to the very spot where they were sure David and his men would be found, lo, nobody was there. Desperately they roamed through the woods in search of them, but all six hundred men had disappeared.

Once more news of Saul's plans had leaked through to David, and he and his men had fled, this time to the nearby wilderness of Maon.

Of course, it wasn't long before Saul found out what had happened, and soon he and his soldiers were in hot pursuit. What a chase it was! For a while the two bodies of men were so close that Saul's soldiers were on one side of a mountain while David and his men were on the other side. At last David's band was completely surrounded, and there seemed no way

36

of escape. "For Saul and his men compassed David and his men round about to take them."

Then the miracle happened.

Suddenly a man appeared over the crest of the mountain, running at top speed toward Saul's soldiers.

Everybody who saw him knew at once that he was a messenger with important tidings.

He was. "Haste thee, and come," he said to the king; "for the Philistines have invaded the land."

The chase was over. At once Saul called his men back from following David, and turned to meet the Philistines.

So once again God came to David's rescue, and he and his men were saved.

STORY 9

Good for Evil

≈≈≈≈≈≈≈≈≈≈≈≈≈≈≈≈≈≈

D AVID and his men now enjoyed a little time of peace, but no sooner had Saul returned from fighting the Philistines than he started off after his most hated enemy again.

This time he took three thousand men with him, and went up into the desolate mountain passes "to seek David and his men upon the rocks of the wild goats."

Day after day they searched, without success. The soldiers looked here, there, and everywhere, but could find no trace of David or any of his men. They had vanished.

Saul was puzzled and annoyed. Where could they be?

One day he turned aside from his soldiers and walked into one of the many caves to be found in that region. It was very dark inside, and the sudden change from the bright sunlight outside made it seem darker still. So Saul did not see who was there.

Unknown to him, this was David's hideout, and the walls

were lined with his men, all with their swords drawn, ready to fight to the death if need be.

Saul was at their mercy, and David knew it. Some of the men whispered to him, "This is your chance, kill him!" But David would not do it. He had no hatred for Saul, only sorrow. Because he was the king, "the Lord's anointed," he would do him no harm.

But the temptation to play a trick on Saul was too great to resist. Noiselessly David crept forward in the darkness until he was so close he could have killed him easily had he wanted to do so. Then, with a quick slash of his dagger, he cut off part of Saul's garment and carried it back to his men.

Then he wished he had not done it. The Bible says that "David's heart smote him, because he had cut off Saul's skirt. And he said unto his men, The Lord forbid that I should do this thing unto my master, the Lord's anointed." But he couldn't put it back.

Meanwhile Saul, having no idea what had happened to him, walked out of the cave and made his way toward his soldiers, who were waiting for him not far away.

Suddenly he heard a shout behind him.

"My lord the king!"

Startled, he turned, and there was David bowing humbly before him.

For a moment he did not know what to say or do. Then David called to him in a tender, pleading voice, "Wherefore hearest thou men's words, saying, Behold, David seeketh thy hurt? . . . Thine eyes have seen how that the Lord had delivered thee to day into mine hand in the cave: and some bade me kill thee: but mine eye spared thee; and I said, I will not put forth mine hand against my lord; for he is the Lord's anointed."

Then he held up the piece of cloth.

"My father," he said, "see, yea, see the skirt of thy robe in my hand: for in that I cut off the skirt of thy robe, and killed thee not, know thou and see that there is neither evil nor transgression in mine hand. . . . The Lord therefore be judge, and judge between me and thee, and see, and plead my cause, and deliver me out of thine hand."

Saul's heart was touched. He began to cry.

"Is this thy voice, my son David?" he said. "Thou art more righteous than I: for thou hast rewarded me good, whereas I have rewarded thee evil."

They talked together for some time, as friendly as in the happy days gone by. Then they bade each other farewell. Saul took his soldiers back home with him, and David and his men returned to their cave.

There was no fighting that day. Nobody was killed and nobody was hurt. People can't fight when somebody returns good for evil as David did.

STORY 10

Brave, Beautiful Abigail

I T MUST have been hard for David to find food for his six hundred men. They could not forever live only on the plants and berries they found in the woods, or even on the birds and wild animals they were able to shoot with their bows and arrows. Now and then they had to ask farmers to help them.

Of course they could have taken food without asking for it, but that was not David's way. He was not a thief or a highwayman. Always he remembered that he had been anointed by the prophet of the Lord as the future king of Israel.

One day he sent ten of his young men to ask for food from a very wealthy farmer named Nabal. This man owned three thousand sheep and a thousand goats, which was a lot of animals in those days. But he was as mean as he was rich.

"Peace be both to thee, and peace be to thine house, and peace be unto all that thou hast," said the young men courteously, as they told Nabal what David wanted.

41

But Nabal happened to be in a very bad mood.

"Who is David?" he snarled. "And who is the son of Jesse? there be many servants now a days that break away every man from his master. Shall I take then my bread, and my water, and my flesh that I have killed for my shearers, and give it unto men, whom I know not whence they be?"

Not a loaf of bread or a drop of water, or even a single kid, would he give to David, and he sent the young men away emptyhanded.

Now it was David's turn to get angry. He had never met such meanness before, and he couldn't take it. So he ordered four hundred of his men to follow him to Nabal's farm, planning to punish the man for his rudeness and selfishness.

But he did not need to get so stirred up. God was still working things out for him as He always had before.

It so happened that Nabal's wife was a very wise woman, besides being very beautiful and brave. When her servants told her how her husband had treated David's ten messengers, she was much upset. And more so when she learned that David's men had long been protecting both her shepherds and her sheep.

At once she wanted to do something to make things right. Without saying a word to Nabal she "made haste, and took two hundred loaves, and two bottles of wine, and five sheep ready dressed, and five measures of parched corn, and an hundred clusters of raisins, and two hundred cakes of figs, and laid them on asses."

That, she knew, would seem a wonderful feast to men who

had been living on wilderness rations for such a long time.

Wisely Abigail sent her servants ahead with the food-laden asses, while she rode behind. Perhaps she remembered how Jacob had once sent presents before him to appease his brother Esau.

When she was part way down the hillside trail, she ran right into David and his men. In a moment they surrounded her and her servants.

The sight of all these fierce-looking men was enough to frighten anybody, certainly a lone woman. But not Abigail. She had expected something like this to happen, and was ready for it. Calmly she got off her donkey and bowed respectfully to David.

Then she pointed to all the food, and explained how this was a present she had brought for his young men.

Anger melted away. Smiles broke out on the faces of those four hundred men at thought of the wonderful meal they would soon enjoy.

43

"Don't take any notice of my husband," she said to David. "Nabal [fool] is his name and folly is with him."

Then, very sweetly, she took all the blame for the misunderstanding upon herself. "I pray thee forgive the trespass of thine handmaid," she said.

What could David do? His heart was touched. He couldn't go and punish this lovely woman's husband now. She was just too sweet and beautiful, and so very gracious!

"Blessed be the Lord God of Israel," he said to her, "which sent thee this day to meet me: and blessed be thy advice, and blessed be thou, which hast kept me this day from coming to shed blood."

Everybody was happy now. Eagerly the men took the food off the asses, and with many thanks went back the way they had come.

Abigail returned home, and finding her husband drunk, told him nothing about what she had done until the morning. When at last she broke the news to him he was so shocked he had a stroke and died a few days later.

When news of Nabal's death reached David, he said, "Blessed be the Lord, that . . . hath kept his servant from evil: for the Lord hath returned the wickedness of Nabal upon his own head." David had taken a great fancy to Abigail, the brave woman who had dared to come alone to meet him when he was angry. So he sent messengers to invite her to come and live with him in the wilderness. Gladly she said Yes, and became his wife.

45

← PAINTING BY HERBERT RUDEEN   © 1955, BY REVIEW AND HERALD
David blessed the Lord when Abigail, wife of wicked Nabal, in return for protection of her husband's herds, brought food to David's four hundred hungry men in the wilderness.

STORY 11

Night Adventure

≈≈≈≈≈≈≈≈≈≈≈≈≈≈

DAVID was now back in the wilderness of Ziph, and one day, to his great surprise, he heard that Saul was coming after him again. He could hardly believe his ears. After what had happened at the cave, when he and the king had had such a friendly chat together, he had thought there would be no more trouble between them. And here was Saul pursuing him again as he had done so many times before.

To make quite sure the story was true, "David . . . sent out spies, and understood that Saul was come in very deed."

Saddened by the news, David wrote the beautiful prayer now found in the fifty-fourth psalm: "Save me, O God, by thy name, and judge me by thy strength. Hear my prayer, O God; give ear to the words of my mouth. . . . Behold, God is mine helper: the Lord is with them that uphold my soul. . . . I will freely sacrifice unto thee: I will praise thy name, O Lord; for it is good."

This time David and his men did not flee. Instead, in the

46

dead of night, they crept toward the place where Saul and his soldiers were encamped.

Closer and closer they moved until they could make out the very place where Saul and Abner, his chief captain, were sleeping.

Saul, they noticed, was in the center of the camp, in the midst of the baggage. Abner was near him, while the rest of the soldiers lay on the ground all around them.

Everyone was fast asleep. Not a sound was to be heard save the snoring of some of the soldiers, the occasional bray of a donkey, or the whinny of a horse.

Suddenly David whispered to two of his bravest men, "Who will go down with me to Saul to the camp?"

"I will," said Abishai.

Without a thought of the terrible risk they were taking, the two brave men crept forward. What if a dog should bark? What if a sentinel should see them? If they should wake the camp, they would not stand a chance.

On they went, careful not to step on any of the sleeping soldiers.

At last they found Saul, sound asleep, his head on a bolster. Beside him was his spear, stuck in the ground, and a cruse, or bottle, of water.

As Abishai looked down at the man who had given David and his men so much trouble, he longed to kill him then and there. "Let me smite him, I pray thee, with the spear even to the earth at once," he whispered to David, "and I will not smite him the second time."

But David would not let him do it. "Destroy him not," he said, "for who can stretch forth his hand against the Lord's anointed, and be guiltless? . . . As the Lord liveth, the Lord shall smite him; or his day shall come to die; and he shall descend into battle, and perish."

So once more he showed his faith in God's leading of his life.

Then, with the same trace of mischief which he had shown in the cave when he cut off part of Saul's garment, he whispered to Abishai, "Take thou now the spear that is at his bolster, and the cruse of water, and let us go."

As silently as they had come, the two men crept out of the camp.

"Then David went over to the other side, and stood on the top of an hill afar off; a great space being between them."

48

It must have been very early in the morning, for when he shouted nobody answered. Everybody in the camp was still asleep.

Then he called again, across the valley, at the top of his voice, "Answerest thou not, Abner?"

Abner got up, very much out of sorts.

"Who art thou that criest to the king?" he roared.

"Art not thou a valiant man?" taunted David. "And who is like to thee in Israel? wherefore hast thou not kept thy lord the king? . . . Now see where the king's spear is, and the cruse of water that was at his bolster."

"Who is it?" I can hear Abner muttering. "What's he talking about?"

But Saul knew David's voice, and called back, "Is this thy voice, my son David?"

"It is my voice, my lord, O king," he said.

Then again he asked the question he had asked so many times before, "What have I done? or what evil is in thine hand?"

When Saul saw his spear and the cruse of water in David's hands, and realized that David must have been by his bed that night, he said, "I have sinned: return, my son David: for I will no more do thee harm, because my soul was precious in thine eyes this day: behold, I have played the fool, and have erred exceedingly."

That was the truest thing Saul ever said. The pity was, he said it too late.

David, as ready as ever to forgive, called back, "Behold the king's spear! and let one of the young men come over and fetch it."

The king was grateful. "Blessed be thou, my son David," he said. "Thou shalt both do great things, and also shalt still prevail."

It was a happy ending to a long quarrel.

David and his men went to Gath, and Saul "sought no more again for him."

STORY 12

The Witch of Endor

ONE REASON why Saul stopped searching for David was because the Philistines were invading the land again.

This time they came in great force, and when Saul saw them he was afraid "and his heart greatly trembled."

He needed advice, but did not know where to go to get it. At other times when he was in trouble he had gone to Samuel, who had always given him counsel from the Lord, but now Samuel was dead.

He would like to have asked the high priest, but he was dead too. He had ordered Doeg, who had charge of his servants, to kill all the priests. Doeg fell upon them with his sword and only Abiathar escaped. Fearing the anger of the king, Abiathar had now fled to David for refuge.

Saul had never felt so lonely and helpless before. He prayed to God, but because of his disobedience God would not answer him.

As the Philistines drew nearer he became desperate. At last he decided to go to a witch and ask her to help him. It was the worst thing he could have done.

In those days a woman who claimed to be able to talk with the dead was called a witch, and because this claim was false, God had said that such people should not be allowed to live in the land. While Samuel was alive Saul had tried to get rid of them, but still a few were left.

Learning that one of these women lived at a place called Endor, the king disguised himself in common clothes and, with two friends, went to visit her.

THE WITCH OF ENDOR

It was night when they arrived, and the witch was afraid that they might be spies who would betray her, but Saul promised solemnly that no harm would come to her if she would only do as he said.

"Whom shall I bring up unto thee?" asked the woman.

"Bring me up Samuel," he said.

Of course she could do no such thing. God would not have let a wicked woman disturb His sleeping prophet. The figure she said she saw was not Samuel, but an evil spirit that looked like Samuel.

As for Saul, he did not see Samuel. He just believed what the woman told him. Then, thinking he was talking to Samuel, he said, "I am sore distressed; for the Philistines make war with me, and God is departed from me, and answereth me no more, neither by prophets, nor by dreams: therefore I have called thee, that thou mayest make known unto me what I shall do."

If Saul thought that he was going to get some good advice, or some encouraging word, he was mistaken. The voice that spoke to him, claiming to be the voice of Samuel, had nothing but evil tidings. Israel, it said, would be defeated in the battle with the Philistines and Saul and his sons would be killed.

Saul came away from the witch of Endor completely discouraged. He had got no help at all. And now he had no heart to fight the Philistines and no strength to plan the war against them. Without hope and without God he could but await the doom he knew was near.

53

Saul's disobedience went so far that when surrounded by the Philistines he sought the counsel of a witch who brought up an evil spirit that pretended he was Samuel the prophet.

STORY 13

Gallant Rescue

MEANWHILE David was having his share of trouble too.

King Achish of Gath had been very kind to him and his men, and had let them make their home in the little town of Ziklag. Happy to have a place they could call their own at last, the six hundred men, with their wives and children, had built up the town and made it prosperous.

Then came the new war between the Philistines and Israel. This was bad for David, because Ziklag and Gath were in the land of the Philistines, and King Achish was expected to use all his able-bodied men in the fight against Israel.

But how could David fight against his own people? No doubt he and his men talked over the problem a long time. What they decided to do the Bible does not say except that, on the day when all the soldiers gathered for the attack, and "the lords of the Philistines passed on by hundreds, and by thousands," David and his men "passed on in the rereward

54

with Achish." Little did they know what was to take place.

Suddenly some princes of the Philistines noticed them.

"What do these Hebrews here?" they demanded.

King Achish told them not to worry. David and his men had been living with him for a long time, he said, and he had found no fault in them.

But the princes would not hear of Hebrews fighting in their ranks against Israel. Angrily pointing at David, they said, "Make this fellow return . . . and let him not go down with us to the battle, lest in the battle he be an adversary to us."

They had a point, and Achish saw it. He called David and begged him to return to Ziklag. "I know that thou art good in my sight, as an angel of God: notwithstanding the princes of the Philistines have said, He shall not go up with us to the battle. Wherefore now rise up early in the morning with thy master's servants that are come with thee: and as soon as ye be up early in the morning, and have light, depart."

There was nothing else David could do. He and his men left for home. And it was a good thing they did. For when they got back to Ziklag they found it burned to the ground.

The Amalekites had attacked the city while the men were all away, and had carried off the women and children and everything David and his men possessed.

It was a terrible shock. They had never dreamed that anything like this would ever happen to them.

"Then David and the people that were with him lifted up their voice and wept, until they had no more power to weep."

What a sad, sad day that was! But the men were not only

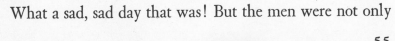

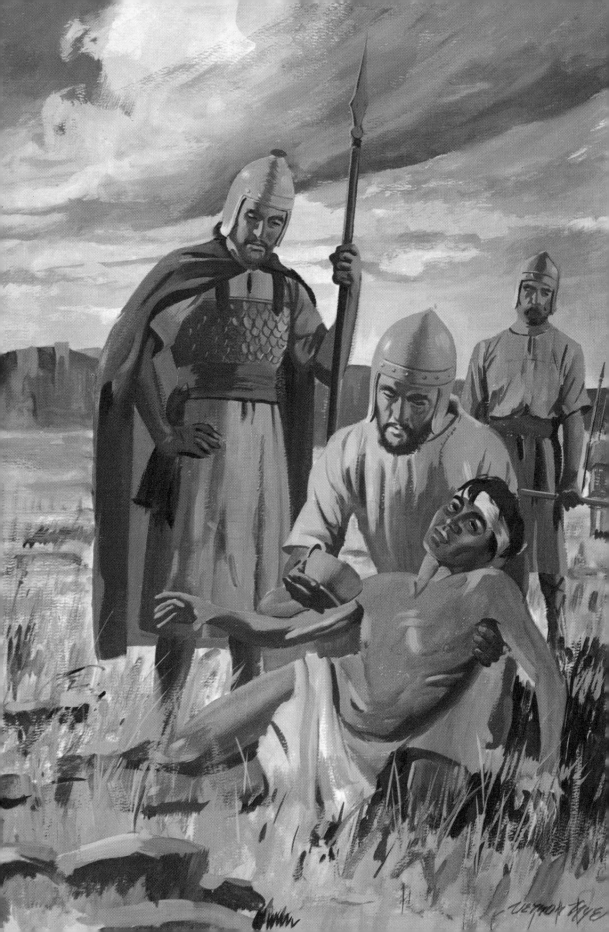

sad, they were angry. Some said that David ought to be stoned, as though it was all his fault. "But David encouraged himself in the Lord his God."

Amid the charred ruins of the city he said to God, "Shall I pursue after this troop? shall I overtake them?"

"Pursue," God said to him, "for thou shalt surely overtake them, and without fail recover all."

David and his men set off after the Amalekites. So hard did they drive themselves that by the time they reached the brook Besor two hundred of them were so tired they could not go a step farther. These were left behind at the brook, with the baggage, while the rest hurried on.

Then they lost their way.

What a trial that must have been when they were so anxious to catch up with the Amalekites before any harm could come to their women and children!

By chance they came across a young Egyptian lad lying in a field. He was sick and faint with hunger, so they gave him some figs and raisins to eat. Pretty soon he was feeling well enough to talk. He said he was a servant of one of the Amalekites who had burned Ziklag. On the way back he had been taken ill, and his master had left him lying in the field.

He told David which way the Amalekites had gone.

This was good news indeed, and soon the four hundred men were on their way again.

That evening they caught up with the enemy, and what a sight they saw! There were the Amalekites "spread abroad upon all the earth, eating and drinking, and dancing, because

57

hile pursuing the Amalekites, David found
ick slave boy left by his master to die on the
ld. He comforted the lad with food, and
e boy told which way the enemy had gone.

of all the great spoil that they had taken out of the land of the Philistines, and out of the land of Judah."

In the midst of the drunken soldiers they saw their wives and children, some of them no doubt bound and shackled.

Suddenly David gave the order to attack, and the four hundred men dashed to the rescue of their loved ones. Furiously they smote the Amalekites "from the twilight even unto the evening of the next day."

How the children must have shouted for joy when they saw their fathers coming to save them! I can almost hear them crying, "Look, Mamma, there's Daddy come to rescue us!"

When the fight was over there was a wonderful reunion as husbands and wives, brothers and sisters, clasped each other in their arms. Everybody was saved. "David recovered all"— all the mothers, all the children, all the flocks, and all the herds, just as God had promised.

For a little while everybody was wildly happy. Then a big argument began.

Some of the men who had gone with David and done the fighting said that the others who had stayed behind at the brook had no right to any of the spoil "save to every man his wife and his children."

But David would have none of it. There was no littleness or meanness in his heart. "Ye shall not do so, my brethren, with that which the Lord hath given us," he said. "As his part is that goeth down to the battle, so shall be his part that tarrieth by the stuff: they shall part alike."

And so they did.

58

STORY 14

Saul's Sad End

IT WAS not long after Saul went to see the witch of Endor that he found himself at the head of his army facing the Philistines.

It was a bad day for Israel. Right from the start of the battle it was as good as lost. With the king himself discouraged, there wasn't a chance of victory. Knowing God was no longer with him, he expected to be defeated, and he was.

Hardly had the fight begun when "the men of Israel fled from before the Philistines." Saul and his sons fled too, with the Philistines hard after them.

First Jonathan was killed, then his two brothers.

Shortly afterward an arrow struck Saul, wounding him badly. Certain that his end was near he asked his armorbearer to kill him. But when the armorbearer would not do it, "Saul took a sword, and fell upon it" and killed himself. Then his armorbearer, seeing his master was dead, "fell upon his sword, and died with him."

Next day, when the battle was over and the Philistines began to strip the slain, they came across the bodies of Saul and his three sons.

They cut off Saul's head and stripped off his armor, and sent it into "the land of the Philistines round about, to publish it in the house of their idols, and among the people."

Later they fastened his body to the wall of the city of Bethshan, put his armor "in the house of their gods, and fastened his head in the temple of Dagon."

It was a terrible end for one who had once been chosen by God to be the first king of Israel.

Why did he die?

The Bible says that "Saul died for his transgression which he committed against the Lord, even against the word of the Lord, which he kept not, and also for asking counsel of one that had a familiar spirit, to enquire of it."

So it was really disobedience that caused his death. Time and again he had disobeyed God, and finally his wrongdoing caught up with him. In going to the witch of Endor he went just one step too far.

Disobeying God is always dangerous. Of course, if we repent and tell Him we are sorry, He will forgive us. But if we go on and on doing things He has told us not to do, the day will come when we may suffer a fate as sad as Saul's.

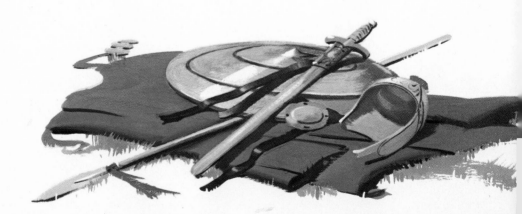

PART II

Stories of the Shepherd King

(2 Samuel 1:1-24:25; 1 Chronicles 1:1-21:30)

STORY 1

Man With a Crown

D AVID had only been back in Ziklag two days after his victory over the Amalekites when news reached him of the death of Saul.

Everybody in the burned-out city had been too busy clearing things up and sorting out the spoil they had taken to give a thought to what might have happened to Israel in their latest battle with the Philistines.

Then came the messenger whose tidings changed all their lives.

David took one glance at him and guessed that he brought bad news, for his clothes were torn and there was earth on his head.

"How went the matter?" David asked him.

Then the man told his story. He had happened to be on Mount Gilboa when Saul was fleeing from the Philistines. He had seen the chariots closing in on him. Then, he said, Saul had called to him and begged that he would kill him.

63

e soldier who brought Saul's crown and
celet to David as proof he had slain the
g was surprised when David turned on him
 taking the life of the Lord's anointed.

"So," said the messenger, "I stood upon him, and slew him, because I was sure that he could not live after that he was fallen: and I took the crown that was upon his head, and the bracelet that was on his arm, and have brought them hither unto my lord."

Then he produced the royal regalia and handed it to David. How everybody must have stared at that crown!

No doubt this messenger thought he would be given a lot of money by David for his boast that he had killed Saul, but he was mistaken.

There was no happiness in Ziklag that day, nor any rejoicing over a fallen foe. Everybody "mourned, and wept, and fasted until even, for Saul, and for Jonathan his son, and for the people of the Lord, and for the house of Israel; because they were fallen by the sword."

The messenger couldn't understand it. Why all this weeping? he wondered. Had he not brought good news? But he had another surprise coming.

Angrily David turned on him, demanding why he was not afraid to destroy the Lord's anointed. Slaying the king was to David a terrible crime.

"Go near and fall upon him," he ordered, and one of his young men killed him on the spot.

Then David, ever the poet, wrote these lines about Saul and Jonathan whom he had loved so much:

64

"The beauty of Israel is slain upon thy high places: how are the mighty fallen!

"Tell it not in Gath, publish it not in the streets of Askelon; lest the daughters of the Philistines rejoice. . . .

"Saul and Jonathan were lovely and pleasant in their lives, and in their death they were not divided: they were swifter than eagles, they were stronger than lions. . . .

"How are the mighty fallen in the midst of the battle! O Jonathan, thou wast slain in thine high places. I am distressed for thee, my brother Jonathan: very pleasant hast thou been unto me: thy love to me was wonderful, passing the love of women.

"How are the mighty fallen, and the weapons of war perished."

So David mourned for Jonathan, and for Saul, too, despite all his unkindness.

No wonder God loved David and said that he was a man after His own heart!

STORY 2

The Field of Strong Men

NEWS of Saul's death raised big questions in David's mind. Should he proclaim himself king, or wait awhile? Should he stay and rebuild Ziklag, or go back and live among his own people in Judah?

As always he took the matter to God.

"Shall I go up into any of the cities of Judah?" he asked.

"Go up," God said.

"Whither shall I go up?"

"Unto Hebron."

Thus simply did David talk with God, ever seeking to do His will.

So he and his men left poor little burned-out Ziklag and went back "every man with his household: and they dwelt in the cities of Hebron."

It was good to be home again. Old friends were so glad to see them after their long exile. In fact, the people of Judah "anointed David king over the house of Judah."

THE FIELD OF STRONG MEN

But David's troubles were not over yet. Abner, the commander in chief of Saul's army, declared that Saul's son Ishbosheth was the rightful heir to the throne, and proclaimed him king of Israel.

So now there were two kings—David, king of Judah, and Ishbosheth, king of Israel.

Both kings had armies. Abner was the commander of one and Joab of the other.

One day these two commanders, with their armies, met by the pool of Gibeon. "And they sat down, the one on the one side of the pool, and the other on the other side of the pool."

How they came to be there we are not told, but by and by Abner said to Joab, "Let the young men now arise, and play for us. And Joab said, Let them arise."

So twelve of the strongest young men in the ranks of David's army went out to meet twelve of the strongest young men in the ranks of Ishbosheth's army.

Those twenty-four fine young men must have made a wonderful sight as they went out to meet strength with strength and valor with valor. But they were so well matched that nobody won. "And they caught every one his fellow by the head, and thrust his sword in his fellow's side; so they fell down together." All twenty-four died and were buried there, and the place was called, "The field of strong men."

Then everybody got into the fight, "and there was a very sore battle that day; and Abner was beaten, and the men of Israel, before the servants of David."

Abner fled for his life, and as he was running away he found himself being followed by Asahel, Joab's brother. He warned the youth not to come too near, but Asahel refused to listen, and Abner struck him with the butt of his spear and killed him—a deed which Joab never forgave.

Abner escaped, but it was the beginning of the end for him. "There was long war between the house of Saul and the house of David: but David waxed stronger and stronger, and the house of Saul waxed weaker and weaker."

God's chosen leader was nearing the throne at last.

STORY 3

Two Mean Tricks

AS WEEKS and months went by Abner saw that his cause was hopeless. David was winning everywhere. Everybody wanted him to be king. So he decided to leave Ishbosheth and join David.

When David heard the news he was very pleased, for he knew this would mean the end of the war. He admired Abner as a strong leader, and believed that he would be as loyal to him as he once was to Saul.

He made one condition of peace—that Abner find Michal, his first wife, and bring her to him. Abner agreed at once, and sent Michal to David. Then he got in touch with all the elders of Israel and told them of his plan to unite the kingdom. "Ye sought for David in times past to be king over you," he said. "Now then do it: for the Lord hath spoken of David, saying, By the hand of my servant David I will save my people Israel out of the hand of the Philistines, and out of the hand of all their enemies."

69

When the elders of Israel had agreed to the plan, Abner sent and told David, who invited him to dinner.

"So Abner came to David to Hebron, and twenty men with him, and David made Abner and the men that were with him a feast."

It was a very happy time. David, bighearted as ever, gladly overlooked all that Abner had done against him in years gone by. Abner, on the other hand, promised to do his best to bring all Israel under David's rule. "I will arise and go," he said, "and will gather all Israel unto my lord the king, that they may make a league with thee, and that thou mayest reign over all that thine heart desireth. And David sent Abner away; and he went in peace."

That could have been the beginning of something very wonderful but, alas, it wasn't.

When Joab heard about what had happened while he was away, he was furious.

"What hast thou done?" he said to David in great anger. "Behold, Abner came unto thee; why is it that thou hast sent him away, and he is quite gone? . . . He came to deceive thee, to know thy going out and thy coming in, and to know all thou doest."

To Joab, Abner was nothing more than a spy; besides, he hated him for killing his brother Asahel.

. Without telling David, he sent messengers after Abner, asking him to return to Hebron.

Supposing that David wanted to see him again, Abner gladly returned, expecting another friendly visit and perhaps another feast. But on his arrival "Joab took him aside in the gate to speak with him quietly, and smote him there under the fifth rib, that he died, for the blood of Asahel his brother."

When David heard about the murder he was horrified. He ordered Joab to put on sackcloth and mourn for the man he had killed. And when the funeral was held "king David himself followed the bier."

To his servants he said, "Know ye not that there is a prince and a great man fallen this day in Israel?"

David was sad and ashamed that one of his own men should have played so mean a trick, and he refused to eat all day. "And all the people took notice of it, and it pleased them: as whatsoever the king did pleased all the people."

Shortly after this, when news of Abner's death spread over the country, two of Saul's captains, Baanah and Rechab, thinking to win David's favor, decided to get rid of Ishbosheth, the rival king.

So one very hot day they came to Ishbosheth's house and found him lying on his bed at noon. They killed him and cut off his head, then carried the head to David, saying to him, "Behold the head of Ishbosheth the son of Saul thine enemy, which sought thy life; and the Lord hath avenged my lord the king this day of Saul, and of his seed."

They could not have made a greater mistake. David was even more angry with them than he had been with Joab.

"As the Lord liveth, who hath redeemed my soul out of all adversity," he said to them, "when one told me, saying, Behold, Saul is dead, thinking to have brought good tidings, I took hold of him, and slew him in Ziklag . . . : how much more, when wicked men have slain a righteous person in his own house upon his bed?"

"And David commanded his young men, and they slew them."

So David let it be known that nothing mean or underhanded would be approved as long as he was king.

STORY 4

David Crowned King

FIFTEEN years had now passed since David killed Goliath, most of which time he had spent hiding from his angry father-in-law. Now he was thirty years of age, and beloved by all the people from one end of the country to the other.

Already he had been anointed king by the people of Judah, but now the rest of Israel, who for a while had remained loyal to Saul's son, wanted to serve him also. "So all the elders of Israel came to the king to Hebron; . . . and they anointed David king over Israel."

What a coronation that was! What a procession! The land of Palestine had never seen anything like it.

Tens of thousands of people came to the ceremony. Every tribe sent its finest troops, all fully armed. And you can be sure their swords and shields and spears were all polished till they shone like mirrors.

At the head of the long line of marching men came the

73

soldiers of Judah—6,800 of them, all bearing shields and spears, "ready armed to the war." Tramp, tramp, tramp!—can't you see them marching by?

Next came 7,100 of the tribe of Simeon, all "mighty men of valour." Then 4,600 of the children of Levi, with 3,700 of the house of Aaron, including Zadok, "a young man mighty of valour" from whose father's house were 22 captains.

Next in line were 3,000 of the men of Benjamin, most of whom had been in the service of Saul till this moment.

HERBERT RUDEEN

Then came a splendid contingent—20,800 of the tribe of Ephraim, all "mighty men of valour, famous throughout the house of their fathers."

Following these were 18,000 from the half tribe of Manasseh, each one "expressly named to come and make David king." (R.S.V.)

Next came 200 older men, sent by the tribe of Issachar. Of them the record says they "had understanding of the times, to know what Israel ought to do."

From Zebulun came 50,000, all marching in perfect precision. They were "expert in war" and "with all instruments of war;" and they could "keep rank: they were not of a double heart."

Naphtali sent 37,000 men and 1,000 captains, all with shields and spears, and these were followed by 28,600 of the men of Dan.

From Asher came 40,000, all keeping their rank.

Then from the tribes living on the other side of Jordan—Reuben, Gad, and half the tribe of Manasseh—came a mighty host numbering 120,000. What a thrilling sight that must have been!

"All these men of war, that could keep rank, came with a perfect heart to Hebron, to make David king over all Israel: and all the rest also of Israel were of one heart to make David king."

After the procession and the coronation there was a great feast, which lasted for three days. Needless to say, a great deal of food was eaten by all those thousands of people. The Bible says that it was prepared by the tribes who lived nearest to Hebron, and they "brought bread on asses, and on camels, and on mules, and on oxen, and meat, meal, cakes of figs, and bunches of raisins, and wine, and oil, and oxen, and sheep abundantly."

Everybody was happy. "There was joy in Israel." It was a wonderful start to David's reign.

Among those present in that great throng were some of David's special friends who had stood by him through all the dark days when he was fleeing from Saul. How they must have enjoyed talking of those exciting times as they ate together!

Outstanding among them were the "three mighties," as they were called, one of whom once fought three hundred men single-handed, and won. Another, in an hour of great peril, had stood shoulder to shoulder with David in a field of barley and turned the tide of battle.

76

DAVID CROWNED KING

Once when they were all hiding in the cave of Adullam, David had said, "Oh that one would give me drink of the water of the well of Bethlehem, that is at the gate!" He longed for some of that clear, cool water he had drunk so often in his boyhood days. Then the "three mighties" had set out to get it for him. Breaking through the ranks of the enemy, they had made their way to the well and brought back some of the water. So overcome had David been by their amazing courage and devotion that he had refused to drink the water, feeling he was unworthy of so great a sacrifice. So, reverently, he had poured it out upon the ground as an offering to God.

Another famous man present at the coronation was Benaiah, who "had done many acts" of great bravery. He could tell of slaying "two lionlike men of Moab," and of slaying a lion in a pit in a snowy day. He once met an Egyptian giant— about eight feet high—who had a spear "like a weaver's beam," and he "plucked the spear out of the Egyptian's hand, and slew him with his own spear."

Together with these great heroes were other "mighty men, helpers of the war." These were armed with bows, and could use both the right hand and the left in hurling stones and shooting arrows out of a bow.

Of still others it is said that they "could handle shield and buckler, whose faces were like the faces of lions, and were as swift as the roes upon the mountains." "One that was least could resist an hundred, and the greatest a thousand."

With such gallant men to help him, no wonder David won the war and came to the throne of Israel!

STORY 5

Jebus Becomes Jerusalem

SOON after David was crowned king of Israel, he decided to take the city of Jebus from the Jebusites and make it the capital of his kingdom.

He knew the place well, for it was only a few miles from Bethlehem, where he was born. No doubt when he was fleeing from Saul he had often wished that he and his men could own as fine a fortress as this.

How long the Jebusites had lived in this "stronghold of Zion" nobody knows, but they were there when Israel invaded Palestine under Joshua. They should have been driven out then, but were not, because the place was too strong.

Having repelled many enemy attacks down the years, the Jebusites felt perfectly safe. They were sure that not even David, with all his valiant men, could take their city. They taunted him by saying that even if everybody in Jebus were blind and lame, he could not capture it, "thinking, David cannot come in hither."

78

JEBUS BECOMES JERUSALEM

But they didn't know David. They forgot that as a boy he might well have been all around the city and learned its ins and outs as only a boy can. It never occurred to them that he might know that the "gutter," or water shaft, was the one weak spot in its defenses—or that David himself might have climbed up it in his youth.

As David planned the attack on the city, he remembered that water shaft and offered to make the first man to climb up it his chief captain.

Joab, David's nephew, offered to lead the way. Others followed him, and the city was taken. Its name was changed to Jerusalem, and it became known as "the city of David."

Happy and proud to be in this famous fortress at last, David began putting up buildings of all kinds for his soldiers and his government. Thus he laid the foundations of the famous city of Jerusalem, which the people of Israel were to look upon as their beloved capital for thousands of years to come.

"And David went on, and grew great, and the Lord God of hosts was with him." The margin of this verse says he "went going and growing," which is a fine thing for any boy or girl to do.

Soon he became known far and wide as a wise and good ruler. Even the famous Hiram, king of Tyre, sent "cedar trees, and carpenters, and masons" to build a house for David, which pleased him very much indeed, for now he saw clearly "that the Lord had established him king over Israel."

The only people who were not pleased were Israel's old enemies, the Philistines. They felt David was becoming too strong. So again they decided to fight Israel, and "spread themselves in the valley of Rephaim."

David wondered what he should do. Then, as of old, he turned to God for advice.

"Shall I go up to the Philistines?" he asked. "Wilt thou deliver them into mine hand?"

"Go up," God said: "for I will doubtless deliver the Philistines into thine hand."

Thus encouraged, he attacked the Philistines, and won a great victory. So quickly did they flee that they "left their images," and David and his men burned them. The sight of those idols lying on the battlefield must have reminded them

of the time when Dagon fell down before the ark of the Lord.

But the Philistines did not accept defeat for long. Soon they launched another attack, and once more David asked God what he should do.

This time God told him exactly how to order the battle. He was not to make an open attack, but to spring a surprise out of a clump of mulberry trees.

Said God, "Let it be, when thou hearest the sound of a going in the tops of the mulberry trees, that then thou shalt bestir thyself: for then shall the Lord go out before thee, to smite the host of the Philistines."

David obeyed exactly. He took his men into the cluster of mulberry trees and hid there, waiting for the promised sign. How they must have watched the slender tops of those mulberry trees! For a long time there was not a sign of movement, only absolute stillness. Some of the men may have wondered whether there was going to be any sign at all.

Then, suddenly, it came. Just a slight fluttering at first, as gentle as if made by the wings of angels. Then more and more, till the tops of the trees were waving madly in the breeze.

With a cheer the men rose from their hiding place and ran to the attack, driving the astonished Philistines before them in headlong flight.

STORY 6

The Ark Comes Home

NOT LONG after his coronation as king of Israel
David talked with the leaders of the nation about
a matter that had been on his heart for some time—
the safety of the ark of God.

In all the trouble between Israel and the Philistines, and
between Saul and David, this sacred chest made of precious
wood and overlaid with gold, containing the Ten Commandments given on Sinai, had been almost forgotten. Certainly it
was no longer the center of worship as it had been in the
wilderness.

After having been taken from the tabernacle by Eli's
wicked sons, Hophni and Phinehas, it had been captured by
the Philistines. Then, after causing them much trouble, it
had been returned to Israel on a cart drawn by two cows. But
it did not get back to the tabernacle. For some years now it
had been at Kirjath-jearim, seven miles from Jerusalem, in the
home of a man called Abinadab.

82

David felt strongly that something so old and so sacred should be properly cared for in the new national capital.

"Let us bring again the ark of our God to us," he said: "for we enquired not at it in the days of Saul."

The leaders of Israel at once agreed to his plan. "The thing was right in the eyes of all the people."

"So David gathered all Israel together, . . . to bring the ark of God from Kirjath-jearim."

Abinadab must have been surprised as he saw the people gathering about his home. Thousands upon thousands came, and at last David himself arrived.

Reverently the ark was carried out of the house and placed on a new cart for the journey to Jerusalem. Uzzah and Ahio, Abinadab's two sons, were given the honor of being the drivers.

As the cart began to move there was a loud burst of music as "David and all Israel played before God with all their might, and with singing, and with harps, and with psalteries, and with timbrels, and with cymbals, and with trumpets."

The singing continued as the great procession made its way toward the City of David. Everybody was so happy. Bringing the ark home seemed to mark the end of all their troubles and the dawn of a new day for Israel. Then suddenly something terrible happened.

As the procession was passing the threshingfloor of Nachon, where the road may have been a little more rough than elsewhere, the oxen stumbled, and the cart tilted. Fearing that the ark might be thrown on the road and damaged, Uzzah put out his hand to steady it—and dropped dead.

All who saw it happen were shocked. Others crowded forward to see the body. The procession stopped, and as the dreadful news was passed back from one to another the singing gradually ceased.

People began to ask why Uzzah had been killed—a question that has been asked over and over again ever since. And the only answer that could be given was that Uzzah knew full well that it was not his place to touch the ark, and that his act of disobedience before so many people, even though well meant, had to be punished severely.

David was very much upset, and decided not to take the ark farther that day. So he had it carried into the home of Obed-edom, and everybody went home.

During the next three months Obed-edom's home was so wonderfully blessed that people heard of it for miles around. When David learned what was taking place, he made up his mind to make one more attempt to bring the ark to Jerusalem.

So another procession was arranged. This time all who were to take part were told to sanctify themselves and put sin out of their lives. Trouble had come the first time, David told

84

them, because "we sought him not after the due order," and he didn't want that to happen again.

After those who carried the ark had gone six paces, David offered up sacrifices. Then, as it moved on once more, he "danced before the Lord with all his might." "So David and all the house of Israel brought up the ark of the Lord with shouting, and with the sound of the trumpet."

Up the steep path they went, through the gate, and into the city. And nobody touched the ark this time, you can be sure.

"And they brought in the ark of the Lord, and set it in his place, in the midst of the tabernacle that David had pitched for it."

Then the choir sang the king's own song, written by David for this great day:

"Give thanks unto the Lord, call upon his name, make known his deeds among the people. Sing unto him, sing psalms unto him, talk ye of all his wondrous works. Glory ye in his holy name: let the heart of them rejoice that seek the Lord. . . .

"Sing unto the Lord, all the earth; shew forth from day to day his salvation. Declare his glory among the heathen; his marvellous works among all nations. . . .

"Blessed be the Lord God of Israel for ever and ever. And all the people said, Amen, and praised the Lord."

So the ark came home at last.

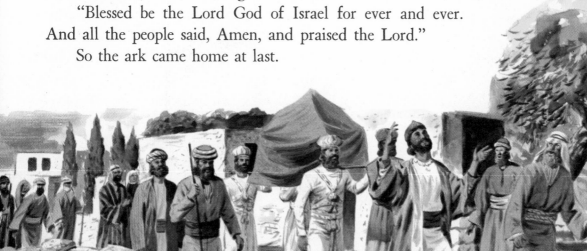

STORY 7

Sitting With the Lord

YEARS went by. David's fine new home was finished. The shepherd boy was now living in a palace. But he wasn't completely happy. Something troubled him. One day he told Nathan the prophet what was on his mind.

"See now," he said to him, "I dwell in an house of cedar, but the ark of God dwelleth within curtains."

He felt that God should have a house far more beautiful than his own, even though he was the king.

That night God spoke to Nathan and told him how pleased He was that David had had this beautiful thought. He gave Nathan a special message for David, which the prophet passed on to him the next day.

"Thus saith the Lord of hosts, I took thee from the sheepcote, from following the sheep, to be ruler over my people, over Israel: and I was with thee whithersoever thou wentest, and have cut off all thine enemies out of thy sight, and have made thee a great name, like unto the name of the great men

86

that are in the earth. . . . And when thy days be fulfilled, and thou shalt sleep with thy fathers, I will set up thy seed after thee, . . . and I will establish his kingdom. He shall build an house for my name, and I will stablish the throne of his kingdom for ever. . . . And thine house and thine kingdom shall be established for ever before thee: thy throne shall be established for ever."

As Nathan told David what God had said about him, the king was deeply moved. At once he went in "and *sat before the Lord,*" probably in the tabernacle, where he had put the ark. Here he bowed humbly before God and thanked Him for all His kindness. His prayer is one of the sweetest in all the Bible.

"Who am I, O Lord God? and what is my house, that thou hast brought me hitherto? . . . And what can David say more unto thee? for thou, Lord God, knowest thy servant. . . . Wherefore thou art great, O Lord God: for there is none like thee, neither is there any God beside thee. . . .

"And now, O Lord God, the word that thou hast spoken concerning thy servant, and concerning his house, establish it for ever, and do as thou hast said. And let thy name be magnified for ever. . . .

"Therefore now let it please thee to bless the house of thy servant, that it may continue for ever before thee: for thou, O Lord God, hast spoken it: and with thy blessing let the house of thy servant be blessed for ever."

So David sat before the Lord and talked with Him, as friend to friend. He did not know, of course, how God planned to fulfill His wonderful promise. He could not see the future, or how it would be through Jesus Christ that his house, his name, and his kingdom would be established forever. He simply trusted God to keep His promise in His own way and in His own good time.

How lovely to talk with God like this! You and I can do it, too. Let us go and sit before the Lord somewhere, just by ourselves, and tell Him all that is in our hearts. If we love Him, as David did, and are as humble and reverent as David was, He will establish our house forever, too. For the promise God made to David that day in the long ago is for all His children, now and always.

STORY 8

"The Kindness of God"

DAVID was always planning some kind deed to do for somebody or other. Maybe that's another reason why God once called him a man after His own heart.

One day, as he was thinking about the days gone by, he remembered his old friend Jonathan, whom he had loved so dearly. What a pity he had been killed in that battle with the Philistines! Had he lived, what good times they could have had together now!

Then David wondered whether there was anybody left belonging to the house of Saul for whom he could do something for Jonathan's sake. As he talked about the matter to his friends, someone suggested that a man called Ziba might know. Not only was he once a servant of Saul's but he now had fifteen sons and twenty servants, and one of them surely would be able to answer the question.

So David sent for Ziba and talked with him.

"Art thou Ziba?" he asked.

"Thy servant," answered the man with a low bow.

"Is there not yet any of the house of Saul, that I may shew the kindness of God unto him?"

"Jonathan hath yet a son," said Ziba, "which is lame on his feet."

Jonathan's son still alive! It didn't seem possible.

"Where is he?" asked David eagerly.

Ziba knew exactly where he was. "He is in the house of Machir, the son of Ammiel, in Lodebar."

Without a moment's delay David sent messengers to Lodebar to fetch Jonathan's son, whose name was Mephibosheth.

When David saw Mephibosheth he felt very sorry for him, for he was lame. The poor man was scared to death, too, feeling sure that there could be no other reason for the royal summons than that David wanted to kill him. So he fell on his face before the king.

But he need not have been afraid.

"Mephibosheth," said David, and there was deep kindness like to love in his voice.

"Behold thy servant," said the man.

"Fear not," said David: "for I will surely shew thee kindness for Jonathan thy father's sake, and will restore thee all the land of Saul thy father; and thou shalt eat bread at my table continually."

Mephibosheth bowed again, hardly able to believe his ears.

"What is thy servant, that thou shouldest look upon such a dead dog as I am?" he said.

David wanted to know how he came to be lame, and

91

When Mephibosheth, the lame son of Jonathan, appeared before the king he trembled with fear, but David was kind to him for Jonathan's sake, and made him a part of the royal household.

learned that the accident happened when he was five years old, on the very day his father Jonathan was killed. When news of Israel's defeat reached the palace, his nurse had picked him up and fled, fearing the Philistines would surely kill him too. In the wild flight to a place of safety, Mephibosheth had fallen and broken both his ankles. Since there was nobody to set them properly, he had become lame for life.

As David listened he became still more sorry for the poor cripple, and gave orders that everything possible should be done for him.

Then he sent for Ziba again and said to him, "I have given unto thy master's son all that pertained to Saul and to all his house. Thou therefore, and thy sons, and thy servants, shall till the land for him, and thou shalt bring in the fruits, that thy master's son may have food to eat: but Mephibosheth thy master's son shall eat bread alway at my table."

Said Ziba, "According to all that my lord the king hath commanded his servant, so shall thy servant do."

Ziba must have been very happy, not only for what had happened to Jonathan's son, but for his own good fortune, too. Caring for all Saul's land was a big job, and meant plenty of work and food for his fifteen sons and twenty servants.

As for Mephibosheth, he was amazed at David's goodness to him. No longer would he live in little out-of-the-way Lodebar, but in Jerusalem. From now on he would eat "at the king's table," and be treated "as one of the king's sons."

What a lovely thing David did out of love for his old friend Jonathan! Surely this was indeed "the kindness of God."

92

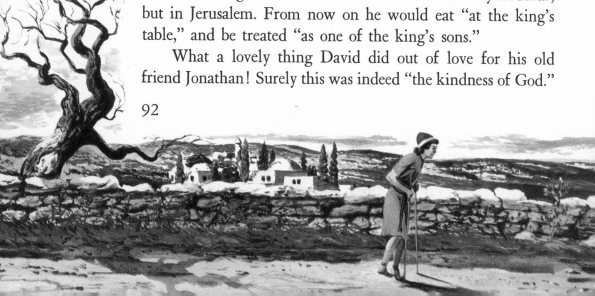

STORY 9

Play the Man!

≋≋≋≋≋≋≋≋≋≋≋≋≋≋≋≋≋≋≋≋≋

NOT ALL of David's kind deeds were appreciated. One of them got him into a lot of trouble.

On learning that the king of Ammon had died, he decided to send some of his servants with a message of sympathy to the family. He wanted the new king Hanun to know that he had not forgotten his father's kindness when he was in hiding from Saul.

But when David's servants arrived in Ammon they were treated as spies, not friends.

Said the princes of Ammon to Hanun, "Thinkest thou that David doth honour thy father, that he hath sent comforters unto thee? hath not David rather sent his servants unto thee, to search the city, and to spy it out, and to overthrow it?"

How suspicious they were! They could not believe that a foreign king could think of doing anything so kind and gracious as to send messengers so far just to express sorrow over an old friend's death.

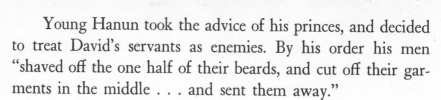

Young Hanun took the advice of his princes, and decided to treat David's servants as enemies. By his order his men "shaved off the one half of their beards, and cut off their garments in the middle . . . and sent them away."

Imagine how ashamed and upset those poor men felt as they returned home! As for David, when he heard what had been done to his messengers he was very angry. He told them to stay at Jericho until their beards had grown before returning to Jerusalem.

Meanwhile Hanun, hearing of David's anger, decided that he had better go to war with Israel, before Israel made war with him. So he sent a thousand talents of silver to Mesopotamia and Syria, and hired 32,000 chariots and horsemen. "And the children of Ammon gathered themselves together from their cities, and came to battle."

"And when David heard of it, he sent Joab, and all the host of the mighty men" to meet them.

With his long experience in war Joab took one look at the armies lined up against him, and decided to take the best of his men and lead them himself against the Syrians, leaving the rest under the command of his brother Abishai to attack the Ammonites.

To Abishai he said, "If the Syrians be too strong for me, then thou shalt help me: but if the children of Ammon be too strong for thee, then I will come and help thee."

PLAY THE MAN!

Then to all his soldiers he gave this glorious message, "Be of good courage, and let us play the men for our people, and for the cities of our God: and the Lord do that which seemeth good."

As the men of Israel went forth to fight that day, then great, challenging words kept ringing in their ears. Every soldier seemed to hear Joab saying to him, "Play the man! Play the man!"

No wonder the Syrians fled! They had no spirit to fight. They were just hired men. But the people of Israel fought like men inspired.

"And when the children of Ammon saw that the Syrians were fled, then they fled also before Abishai" until they reached the safety of their fortress of Rabbah.

So the Ammonites lost the battle and their thousand talents of silver, as well as the friendship of Israel. And all because of their foolishness in treating the servants of David so rudely.

STORY 10

A Shadow Falls

THERE was a sad ending to the story of the defeat of the Ammonites.

Early the following year David sent Joab with all the men of Israel to lay siege to their capital city, Rabbah. He knew that Israel could never feel safe again until it was taken.

For once he did not go with his army to battle, but stayed home with his family. And then it was that a dark shadow fell upon Jerusalem and its king.

Up to this moment David had been everywhere as a good and noble man. People thought of him as a champion of right and truth. They were glad that at last there was a man on the throne who was loyal to the God of heaven. They loved him for what he had done to revive the holy religion of their fathers, and for honoring God's law by bringing back the ark.

Because of all this, and because of his kind and generous heart, God had blessed him greatly. Through many dangers and perils He had brought him from the sheepfold to the

96

throne, from poverty to plenty, and had given him houses and lands and gold and silver in abundance.

David was now king over all the land from Egypt to the Euphrates, so that in him God had fulfilled His promise to Abraham, "Unto thy seed have I given this land, from the river of Egypt unto the great river, the river Euphrates." Genesis 15:18.

As was the custom in those days, David had many wives and lots of children. Indeed, his house must have been over-run with boys and girls who called him Father. Surely, one would think, he had enough to make and keep him happy. But no. As too often happens with those to whom God has given much, he wanted more—something he well knew he should not have.

Nobody likes to tell the story, yet it must be told. While the army was away at Rabbah, David fell in love with the wife of Uriah the Hittite, one of his finest and noblest soldiers. Then, to make matters worse, he wrote a letter to Joab, order-ing him to put Uriah "in the forefront of the hottest battle" so that he would be killed. And he asked Uriah to carry the letter—his own death warrant!

And that shows how one mean thing leads to another.

Imagine what Joab must have thought when he received such a letter from the king! Surely he must have wondered

what had gone wrong. Yet he obeyed his master. Uriah was sent up close to the wall of Rabbah, where "the valiant men were," and in the course of the fighting met his death.

When David heard the news, he thought his little plot had succeeded very well. He was sure nobody would ever find out what he had done. He waited awhile until Uriah's wife, Bathsheba, had mourned for her husband, then sent for her and married her. What could be more proper?

But if David thought that God did not know what he had done, or did not care, he was much mistaken.

God knew all about it and was deeply disappointed. The Bible says that "the thing that David had done displeased the Lord."

It was a terrible letdown. If any ordinary man had done such a thing, it would have been bad enough; but for the king to do it—who should have been an example to his people —that was awful. After all that David had said about keeping the Ten Commandments, he had broken them all at once himself! By so doing he had "given great occasion to the enemies of the Lord to blaspheme."

So the shadow of a great sin fell over David and his family, and over Jerusalem and all Israel.

≈≈≈≈≈≈

STORY 11

David's Repentance

≈≈≈≈≈≈≈≈≈≈≈≈≈≈≈≈≈≈

FOR A WHILE David tried to live as though he had done nothing wrong. After all, he told himself, Uriah had died in battle, hadn't he? Wasn't it perfectly all right for somebody else to marry the poor man's widow? Anyway, nobody knew the truth. Joab might be suspicious, but he had no proof.

But David's conscience bothered him. It gave him no rest, night or day.

Then one day Nathan the prophet came to see him, and told him a story.

"There were two men in one city," he said; "the one rich, and the other poor. The rich man had exceeding many flocks and herds: but the poor man had nothing, save one little ewe lamb, which he had bought and nourished up: and it grew up together with him, and with his children. . . .

"And there came a traveller unto the rich man, and he spared to take of his own flock and of his own herd, to dress

99

for the wayfaring man who was come unto him; but took the poor man's lamb, and dressed it."

As David listened he became very angry. The rich man's injustice shocked him.

"As the Lord liveth," he exploded, "the man that hath done this thing shall surely die: and he shall restore the lamb fourfold, because he did this thing, and because he had no pity."

Suddenly the prophet, pointing at the king, cried, "Thou art the man!"

David turned pale. His secret was known!

"Thus saith the Lord God of Israel," Nathan went on, "I anointed thee king over Israel, and I delivered thee out of the hand of Saul; and I gave thee . . . the house of Israel and of Judah; and if that had been too little, I would moreover have given unto thee such and such things.

"Wherefore hast thou despised the commandment of the Lord, to do evil in his sight? thou hast killed Uriah the Hittite with the sword, and hast taken his wife to be thy wife, and hast slain him with the sword of the children of Ammon."

So God knew all about it! Every horrid detail! What would his punishment be?

"Thus saith the Lord," Nathan went on, "Behold, I will raise up evil against thee out of thine own house, and I will take thy wives before thine eyes, and give them unto thy neighbour. . . . For thou didst it secretly: but I will do this thing before all Israel, and before the sun."

David was crushed. In great grief he cried, "I have sinned against the Lord."

100

Suddenly he saw how very, very wicked he had been, how great a sin he had committed. Falling upon his knees, he cried, with tears, "Have mercy upon me, O God, according to thy lovingkindness: according unto the multitude of thy tender mercies blot out my transgressions. Wash me throughly from mine iniquity, and cleanse me from my sin. For I acknowledge my transgressions: and my sin is ever before me. Against thee, thee only, have I sinned, and done this evil in thy sight. . . .

"Purge me with hyssop, and I shall be clean: wash me, and I shall be whiter than snow. . . . Hide thy face from my sins, and blot out all mine iniquities. Create in me a clean heart, O God; and renew a right spirit within me. Cast me not away from thy presence; and take not thy holy spirit from me. Restore unto me the joy of thy salvation; and uphold me with thy free spirit. . . .

"The sacrifices of God are a broken spirit: a broken and a contrite heart, O God, thou wilt not despise."

God heard David's prayer and, great as was his sin, He

101

forgave him. Right then and there He said through Nathan, "The Lord also hath put away thy sin; thou shalt not die."

How kind and patient the Lord is with those who repent of their sins! However great the wrong we may have done, if we are really sorry, and tell Him so, He will put it away and cast it behind His back. For, wonder of wonders, "if we confess our sins, he is faithful and just to forgive us our sins, and to cleanse us from all unrighteousness." 1 John 1:9.

Yet even though God forgave David for that evil thing he did, He could not stop the consequences of it—to David, his family, and his kingdom.

That sin was the dividing point in his life. Before it he seemed to be getting stronger and stronger. After it he became weaker and weaker. Things were never the same again. He lost the respect of many of his people and of his own children. He was afraid to rebuke them for wrongdoing for fear they would say, What about you?

That is what sin does. It weakens. It divides. It spoils everything it touches. It takes the joy and the beauty out of life.

How true it is that the bird with the broken pinion never flies so high again!

STORY 12

A Very Bad Boy

AMONG David's many sons there was one who stood out above all the others. He was so good looking and had such winning ways.

His name was Absalom, and the Bible says of him that "in all Israel there was none to be so much praised as Absalom for his beauty: from the sole of his foot to the crown of his head there was no blemish in him."

But his beauty was all on the outside. In his heart, which nobody could see, were pride, envy, hatred, and many other unlovely things.

Once he invited all of his brothers to a picnic at the time of the shearing of the sheep. All of them went, but they did not all return.

When the boys got back to Jerusalem that night, two were missing. Amnon was dead and Absalom, who had killed him, had fled, fearing his father's anger.

Absalom stayed away from home for three long years.

103

Only through the kindness of Joab, who pleaded with David to recall him, was he able to return even then.

When at last he arrived home, he might have been expected to show some gratitude to Joab, but no. Instead, when Joab did not come to see him when this impatient youth thought he should, he burned one of Joab's fields of barley out of spite.

It was five years after the murder of Amnon before Absalom saw his father again. That must have been a touching meeting. Ever tenderhearted, David forgave him for the great wrong he had done, and kissed him.

Was Absalom grateful that his life had been spared?

Not at all. Instead, he began to plan a rebellion that would put him on the throne.

As a first step he prepared chariots and horses "and fifty men to run before him," so people would know how important he was. Then he began to go early every day to the main gate of the city, where he talked kindly to all the important people who came in and out. He would ask them how far they had come, and what they planned to do in Jerusalem. If a man said he had a case he wished to take to the king for judgment, Absalom would say, "Thy matters are good and right; but there is no man deputed of the king to hear thee. . . . Oh that I were made judge in the land, that every man which hath any suit or cause might come unto me, and I would do him justice!"

Thus he spread the idea abroad that he would make a better king than his father.

When a man bowed to him he would put his arms around
him and kiss him. So he was known and loved as a kind and
sympathetic leader.

"So Absalom stole the hearts of the men of Israel."

When he thought he had stolen enough hearts to gain
the kingdom, he sent messengers secretly through all the land
of Israel saying, "As soon as ye hear the sound of the trumpet,
then ye shall say, Absalom reigneth in Hebron."

So did this very bad boy plot against his father. "And
the conspiracy was strong; for the people increased continually
with Absalom."

How many went to Hebron when Absalom set himself up as king, we are not told; but it must have been a very large number, because when a messenger arrived with the news of the rebellion, David said to all his faithful friends in Jerusalem, "Arise, and let us flee; for we shall not else escape from Absalom: make speed to depart, lest he overtake us suddenly, . . . and smite the city with the edge of the sword."

The last thing David wanted was to have his beloved Jerusalem turned into a battlefield. So with a heavy heart he decided to leave the city.

What a sad, sad day that was! The Bible says that everybody was in tears. "All the country wept with a loud voice." As for David, as he "went up by the ascent of mount Olivet" he "wept . . . and had his head covered, and he went barefoot: and all the people that was with him covered every man his head, and they went up, weeping as they went up."

So David, who had spent so much of his life fleeing from his father-in-law, now fled in fear and sorrow from one of his own sons.

STORY 13

Two Boys in a Well

IN THAT hour of his great sorrow David discovered who his real friends were.

As the crowds of people poured out of the gates of Jerusalem—men and women, boys and girls—all fleeing from Absalom, the weeping king noticed that the chief priests, Abiathar and Zadok, were among them, bearing the ark of God. Their sons Jonathan and Ahimaaz were there, too. David stopped and spoke to them.

"Carry the ark of God into the city," he told them. "If I shall find favour in the eyes of the Lord, he will bring me again." Then he made his way to the wilderness.

Meanwhile Absalom entered Jerusalem with his army, and took over his father's palace. Calling his wisest men he asked what he should do next. One of them, Ahithophel, advised that David should be pursued at once and taken; but Hushai the Archite, David's old friend, tried to delay things. Anxious to give David time to escape, he advised Absalom to wait until he could get all the men of Israel together, and then go after David; and the council thought that Hushai's plan was the better one.

When the meeting was over, Hushai went to Abiathar and Zadok the priests, and told them to send word at once to David to escape over the Jordan while he still had time to do so.

To avoid arousing suspicion, the priests asked a young girl to take the message to their two sons, Jonathan and Ahimaaz, who were staying in a village outside Jerusalem. She did so, but "a lad saw them and told Absalom."

Jonathan and Ahimaaz must have seen that lad listening, and guessed they were in for trouble, for they hurried away quickly, looking for a place to hide. As they ran for dear life they remembered that in the yard of a friend's home there was a well. They made for it and climbed down, just in time. The woman of the house put a large cloth over the top of the well and spread ground corn on it.

Soon the two boys heard the shouts of Absalom's men in the yard above them.

But the woman did not betray them.

When the soldiers had gone on their way, Ahimaaz and Jonathan climbed up out of the well and hurried to David.

It was still dark when the boys arrived, but David acted at once. He ordered everybody to the riverbank—men, women, and children. Some swam across, others used the "ferry boat" (2 Samuel 19:18), but "by the morning light there lacked not one of them that was not gone over Jordan."

So David and his friends escaped.

108

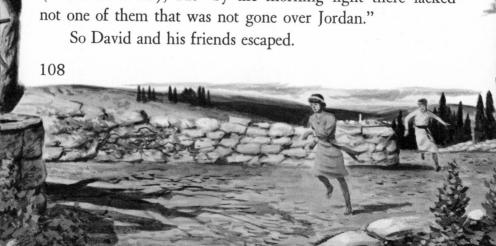

STORY 14

Caught in a Tree

O N THE other side of Jordan, David found many more friends who were sorry for him and wanted to help him.

One group "brought beds, and basons, and earthen vessels, and wheat, and barley, and flour, and parched corn, and beans, and lentiles, and parched pulse, and honey, and butter, and cheese of kine, for David and for the people that were with him, to eat: for they said, The people is hungry, and weary, and thirsty, in the wilderness."

Refreshed, David and his followers went on to the city of Mahanaim.

Here more and more men came to join his army. Soon he had several thousand of the finest soldiers in Israel with him, and was ready to meet Absalom when he should come to attack him.

At last the day of battle came. Strangely, on that very morning, as the men of war were marching out of the city gate, David said to them, "Deal gently for my sake with the young man, even with Absalom." Even yet he loved the boy, despite all the evil he had done.

David wanted to lead his men into battle as of old, but they refused to let him. "Thou art worth ten thousand of us," they said: "therefore now it is better that thou succour us out of the city."

So David stayed behind, sitting at the city gate waiting impatiently for news.

Absalom's army did not stand a chance against David's seasoned warriors. It was soon scattered and destroyed.

Fleeing on a mule, Absalom met with a strange accident. As he was passing under a great oak in the forest of Ephraim, his head caught in the boughs of the tree. A forked branch gripped him by the neck; and as his mule dashed away from under him, he was left dangling helplessly in the air.

One of David's men found Absalom in the tree and ran to tell Joab.

Nothing could have pleased Joab more. He had many a score to settle with this young man. Forgetting David's request to "deal gently" with him, he thrust three darts through his heart. Then he had Absalom's body thrown into a deep pit and covered with stones.

Meanwhile David was still waiting for news at the city gate. By and by the watchman on the wall above cried, "I see a man running alone."

"If he be alone," said the king, "there is tidings in his mouth."

Then to David's surprise the watchman cried, "I see another man running alone."

"He also bringeth tidings," said the king, hardly able to wait for one of the messengers to arrive.

As the first runner came nearer and nearer the watchman called from the wall, "Me thinketh the running of the foremost is like the running of Ahimaaz the son of Zadok"—one of the boys who hid in the well!

"He is a good man," said the king, "and cometh with good tidings."

As Ahimaaz reached the king he panted, "All is well," and fell down, exhausted.

"Is the young man Absalom safe?" asked David eagerly.

"I saw a great tumult, but I knew not what it was," said the young man, fearing to tell the king the truth.

"Turn aside, and stand here," said David, as the second runner arrived.

"Tidings, my lord the king," cried Cushi: "for the Lord hath avenged thee this day of all them that rose up against thee."

"Is the young man Absalom safe?" asked David anxiously.

Said Cushi, "The enemies of my lord the king, and all that rise against thee to do thee hurt, be as that young man is."

David guessed what had happened and was heartbroken. He had hoped for victory, of course, but not at so great a price. Bursting into tears, he went up to the room over the city gate, crying, "O my son Absalom, my son, my son Absalom! would God I had died for thee, O Absalom, my son, my son!"

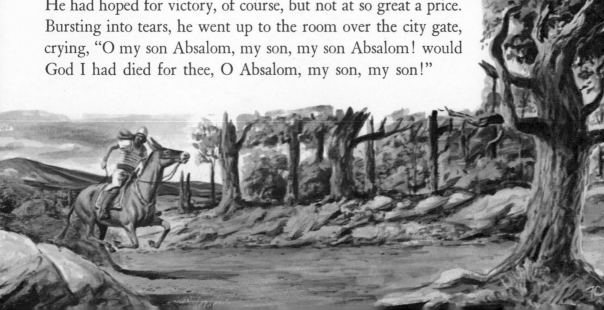

STORY 15

Angel Over Jerusalem

DAVID waited awhile in Mahanaim until the trouble over Absalom had died down. Then, using the ferry boat again, he and his men crossed the Jordan once more and climbed up the steep mountain trail to Jerusalem.

As they neared Jerusalem, Mephibosheth, Jonathan's lame son, came to meet David. He was looking very untidy, for he "had neither dressed his feet, nor trimmed his beard, nor washed his clothes, from the day the king departed until the day he came again in peace." He tried to explain that it was only his lameness that had kept him from going with David when he fled from Jerusalem.

At last the long column reached the "stronghold of Zion." So happy was David to be back home again that he composed this beautiful psalm:

"The Lord is my rock, and my fortress, and my deliverer; the God of my rock; in him will I trust: he is my shield, and the horn of my salvation, my high tower, and my refuge, my saviour. . . .

4-8

Delivered now from Saul and all his enemies, David sang: "The Lord is my rock and my fortress, and my deliverer; the God of my rock . . my high tower, and my refuge, my saviour."

"For thou art my lamp, O Lord: and the Lord will lighten my darkness. . . .

"For who is God, save the Lord? and who is a rock, save our God? God is my strength and power: and he maketh my way perfect."

Restored to the throne, David sought for ways to make himself strong. Forgetting that God was "his strength and power," he decided to follow the custom of the heathen nations about him by building up a big military force.

With this in mind he said to Joab, "Go, number Israel . . . ; and bring the number of them to me, that I may know it."

Even Joab, hardened soldier though he was, believed David was making a mistake.

"The Lord make his people an hundred times so many more as they be," he said, "but, my lord the king, are they not all my lord's servants? why then doth my lord require this thing? why will he be a cause of trespass to Israel?"

But David was obstinate. He insisted that the numbering be done.

Joab did as he was told. Some time later he came back with the figures. In all Israel and Judah, he said, there were 1,570,000 men "that drew sword."

Hardly had Joab left him than David realized what he had done. Turning to God, he said, "I have sinned greatly, because I have done this thing: but now, I beseech thee, do away the iniquity of thy servant: for I have done very foolishly."

Soon a prophet named Gad came to see David, and told him that there was a price to pay for his sin, but he could

114

choose his own punishment. It could be three *years* of famine, three *months* of invasion by a foreign foe, or three *days* of pestilence, with "the angel of the Lord destroying throughout all the coasts of Israel."

It was a hard decision to make, but finally David said, "Let me fall now into the hand of the Lord; for very great are his mercies: but let me not fall into the hand of man."

So a great pestilence came upon Israel and many people died. The number of men Joab had counted was reduced by seventy thousand.

Then it was that David saw the dreadful vision of the angel of the Lord over Jerusalem, his beloved city.

He was standing "between the earth and the heaven," by the threshingfloor of Ornan the Jebusite, and he had "a drawn sword in his hand stretched out over Jerusalem."

"Then David and the elders of Israel, who were clothed in sackcloth, fell upon their faces."

Pleading with God to spare the people of Jerusalem, David took all the blame upon himself, crying, "Is it not I that commanded the people to be numbered? even I it is that have sinned and done evil indeed; but as for these sheep, what have they done? let thy hand I pray thee, O Lord my God, be on me, and on my father's house; but not on thy people, that they should be plagued."

At once there came a message from God through the prophet Gad telling him to go to the threshingfloor of Ornan and build an altar there. He went.

Ornan had been threshing wheat, but when he and his four sons had seen the angel they had hid themselves. Still trembling, they came out to meet the worried, sad-faced king.

When David asked if he could buy the place so that he might build an altar there, Ornan generously replied, "Take it to thee . . . : I give thee the oxen also for burnt offerings, and the threshing instruments for wood, and the wheat for the meat offering; I give it all."

No, said David, "I will verily buy it for the full price: for I will not take that which is thine for the Lord, nor offer burnt offerings without cost."

David paid Ornan six hundred shekels of gold for everything. Then he built an altar and laid a sacrifice on it.

Suddenly there was a flash of fire from heaven, and the sacrifice was consumed in flame and smoke.

David knew then that God had forgiven him again.

So the pestilence ended, and the angel with the sword was seen no more.

PART III

Stories of Solomon
(1 Kings 1:1-11:43)

STORY 1

The Interrupted Party

D AVID was getting to be quite an old man now, almost seventy years of age. Although his mind was still keen, he was beginning to feel the effects of his long, hard life.

No longer could he lead his men into battle as he had done in years gone by; no more could he go for long marches over the mountains as once he had done with ease.

More and more he had to stay around home. Then he had to take to his bed. But he wasn't finished yet.

There was one thing more he wanted to do. Truly repentant for all his sins, he yearned to render God one last service. His plan was to build a beautiful temple for the worship of God, a place where the precious ark would be safe. He knew he could never finish such a temple in what was left of his lifetime, but at least he could start it.

So he gave orders that masons should start hewing great stones "to build the house of God." He also "prepared iron

119

← PAINTING BY HARRY ANDERSON   © 1955, BY REVIEW AND HERALD

By divine appointment David, at the height of his glory, was proclaimed king of Israel, and through the royal "house of David" was to come Christ, the Messiah, the Saviour of men.

in abundance for the nails for the doors of the gates, and for the joinings; and brass in abundance without weight; also cedar trees in abundance."

Week by week and month by month the supplies poured in, and as reports of the growing piles of stone, lumber, brass, and iron reached the aging king, his old heart was filled with joy. How he wished he might live a few more years and build the temple himself!

But this could not be, for his days were numbered. His son Solomon would have to carry on where he left off.

"Solomon my son is young and inexperienced," he said to himself, "and the house that is to be built for the Lord must be exceedingly magnificent, of fame and glory throughout all lands; I will therefore make preparation for it."

"So David provided materials in great quantity before his death."

But everybody did not know that it was his plan to have Solomon reign after him. Among his many sons there was a good deal of talk about which of them should wear the royal crown when Father was dead. One of them, Adonijah, made up his mind that the throne should be his. "I will be king," he told himself and—just as Absalom had done years before—he "prepared him chariots and horsemen, and fifty men to run before him."

Being a fine-looking lad, he made quite an impression upon some people. Even Joab, general of the army, and Abiathar, the old high priest, decided that he was the one to succeed David.

120

Encouraged by such strong support, Adonijah made a great feast and called his brothers and many of the king's servants to sit with him and hear him proclaimed king.

David, of course, knew nothing of all this. He was in bed, dreaming of the temple he wanted to build.

Suddenly Bathsheba, the mother of Solomon, burst into his room, very much upset.

"My lord," she cried, "thou swarest by the Lord thy God unto thine handmaid, saying, Assuredly Solomon thy son shall reign after me, and he shall sit upon my throne. And now, behold, Adonijah reigneth; and now, my lord the king, thou knowest it not: and he hath slain oxen and fat cattle and sheep in abundance, and hath called all the sons of the king, and Abiathar the priest, and Joab the captain of the host: but Solomon thy servant hath he not called. And thou, my lord, O king, the eyes of all Israel are upon thee, that thou shouldest tell them who shall sit on the throne of my lord the king after him."

The sick, weary king stirred on his bed. The old light came back into his eyes. Nobody was going to do this to him! But before he could speak, in came Nathan the prophet.

He told the same story as Bathsheba had, and asked, "My lord, O king, hast thou said, Adonijah shall reign after me, and he shall sit upon my throne?"

Quickly the old king made his decision.

"Call Bathsheba," he said, and she came near him.

"As the Lord liveth," he said to her, "that hath redeemed my soul out of all distress, even as I sware unto thee by the Lord God of Israel, saying, Assuredly Solomon thy son shall reign after me, and he shall sit upon my throne in my stead; even so will I certainly do this day."

Next he called Zadok the priest and Nathan the prophet, and told them to anoint Solomon king of Israel, then put him on the royal mule and lead him through Jerusalem crying, "God save King Solomon!"

These men did as they were told, and when the people saw the young man riding on David's mule, they guessed what had happened, and shouted aloud in their happiness. The Bible says they "rejoiced with great joy, so that the earth rent

with the sound of them" as they cried out again and again, "God save King Solomon!"

Meanwhile Adonijah and his friends were just finishing their feast. As the guests were sitting around talking about what they should do next, they heard the commotion in Jerusalem. What could it mean? they wondered. Joab, the old warrior, was worried most. "Wherefore is this noise of the city being in an uproar?" he asked anxiously.

He soon found out; for at that moment Jonathan, son of Abiathar, the high priest, came running with the big news that David had abdicated in favor of Solomon.

"And Zadok the priest and Nathan the prophet have anointed him king in Gihon," he gasped out, "and they are come up from thence rejoicing, so that the city rang again. This is the noise that ye have heard. And also Solomon sitteth on the throne of the kingdom."

Suddenly the party was forgotten. Quickly the guests disappeared, fleeing for their lives lest the friends of Solomon should find them.

123

STORY 2

David's Glorious Farewell

WHEN David felt that his end was near, he had a great desire to speak to the leaders of Israel once more, as he had so many times in the past. So he sent messengers all over the country to call together "all the princes of Israel, . . . and the captains of the companies . . . , and the captains over the thousands, and captains over the hundreds, and the stewards over all the substance and possession of the king, and of his sons, with the officers, and with the mighty men, and with all the valiant men, unto Jerusalem."

Many of these leaders were his old friends. Some of the "mighty men" and the "valiant men" had stood by him through the dark days when he fled before King Saul. They had grown old together, and now the day of parting was drawing near. Anxiously they hurried toward Jerusalem, wondering what they would find when they arrived.

All knew that David had been bedridden for some time, and that he was growing weaker every passing month. They

124

anxiously wondered if this would be the very last time they would see him.

One by one they filed into the crowded meeting place, their faces grave and worried. Presently David was brought in, perhaps on a couch or bed. How good it was to see him again! Yet how sad that their once mighty leader was now so old and feeble!

But there was no accounting for David. He seemed to have secret reserves of strength for every emergency. Again and again through his long, danger-filled life he had surprised both friends and enemies in times of seeming defeat. Now it happened again. Suddenly the old king rallied. Rising to his feet, he began to speak with much of the power and authority of other days.

"Hear me, my brethren, and my people," said the grand old man. "As for me, I had in mine heart to build an house of rest for the ark of the covenant of the Lord, and for the footstool of our God, and had made ready for the building: but God said unto me, Thou shalt not build a house for my name, because thou hast been a man of war, and hast shed blood. . . .

125

"And of all my sons, (for the Lord hath given me many sons,) he hath chosen Solomon my son to sit upon the throne of the kingdom of the Lord over Israel.

"And he said unto me, Solomon thy son, he shall build my house and my courts: for I have chosen him to be my son, and I will be his father. Moreover I will establish his kingdom for ever, if he be constant to do my commandments and my judgments, as at this day.

"Now therefore in the sight of all Israel the congregation of the Lord, and in the audience of our God, keep and seek for all the commandments of the Lord your God: that ye may possess this good land, and leave it for an inheritance for your children after you for ever."

Then, turning to his son Solomon, who no doubt was close by him, he said, before all the people, "And thou, Solomon my son, know thou the God of thy father, and serve him with a perfect heart and with a willing mind; for the Lord searcheth all hearts, and understandeth all the imaginations of the thoughts: if thou seek him, he will be found of thee; but if thou forsake him, he will cast thee off for ever.

"Take heed now; for the Lord hath chosen thee to build an house for the sanctuary: be strong, and do it."

Then David handed over to his son the blueprints which he had prepared for every detail of the great and beautiful building he had planned. Included were patterns of "the porch, . . . and of the treasuries . . . and of the upper chambers . . . and of the inner parlors . . . and of the place of the mercy seat," and much, much more.

"All this," said David, "the Lord made me understand in writing by his hand upon me, even all the works of this pattern."

Everybody must have been astonished at these words. Few of those present could have had any idea that all the plans were ready for the new temple, or that God had dictated them personally to the king. This was just like what had happened centuries before on Mount Sinai, when God showed Moses the pattern of the wilderness tabernacle!

Turning now to the congregation once more, David told of all the other preparations he had made for the building and of the stores of gold, silver, brass, iron, wood, and precious stones he had gathered together.

Then he revealed his own personal gift—the last gift he would ever be able to make to God—"three thousand talents of gold . . . , and seven thousand talents of refined silver."

At this all hearts were deeply touched. What a magnificent gift was this from their beloved leader, old, weak, and dying though he was! It was hard for some to keep from weeping.

A moment later something wonderful began to happen.

127

One by one the leaders of Israel came forward with their own rich gifts and pledges of gold, silver, brass, iron, and precious stones.

Nothing like this had been seen since that day in the wilderness when the people brought their treasures to Moses to build the tabernacle.

It seemed as though everybody present wanted to have some part in helping to make the old king's dream come true. Gladly they brought him the best they had, rejoicing at the look of gratitude and happiness on his dear old face.

"Then the people rejoiced, for that they offered willingly, because with perfect heart they offered willingly to the Lord; and David the king also rejoiced with great joy."

When the last of the people had presented their offerings, David blessed the Lord before the whole congregation. Using some of the most beautiful words to be found in all the Bible, he said:

"Blessed be thou, Lord God of Israel our father, for ever and ever. Thine, O Lord, is the greatness, and the power, and the glory, and the victory, and the majesty: for all that is in the heaven and in the earth is thine; thine is the kingdom, O Lord, and thou art exalted as head above all. . . . Now therefore, our God, we thank thee, and praise thy glorious name. . . .

"O Lord our God, all this store that we have prepared to build thee an house for thine holy name cometh of thine hand, and is all thine own. . . . O Lord God of Abraham, Isaac, and of Israel, our fathers, keep this for ever in the imagination of

128

the thoughts of the heart of thy people, and prepare their heart unto thee."

Then, so tenderly, he prayed for his son. "Give unto Solomon my son a perfect heart, to keep thy commandments, thy testimonies, and thy statutes, and to do all these things, and to build the palace, for the which I have made provision."

"Now bless the Lord your God," he said to the congregation, and, together with the old king, they bowed their heads and worshiped.

It was a noble and glorious finish to the life of a man who, despite his many mistakes, had tried to serve God the best he knew how.

4-9

STORY 3

Solomon's Prayer for Wisdom

THE VERY next day after David had made his last speech to his people, a great feast was held in Jerusalem, and Solomon was made king for the second time.

Most of the leaders of Israel had not been present when David had sent Solomon through the city on his royal mule at the time Adonijah tried to seize the throne. So now that they were all in the city to bid farewell to their old king, it was thought best to have another coronation. So they "made Solomon the son of David king the second time, and anointed him unto the Lord to be the chief governor. . . . Then Solomon sat on the throne of the Lord as king instead of David his father, and prospered; and all Israel obeyed him.

"And all the princes, and the mighty men, and all the sons likewise of king David, submitted themselves unto Solomon the king.

"And the Lord magnified Solomon exceedingly in the sight of all Israel, and bestowed upon him such royal majesty as had not been on any king before him in Israel."

130

SOLOMON'S PRAYER FOR WISDOM

There was a reason why God conferred high honor and great blessing upon this young man: he was so eager to do right.

Soon after his coronation Solomon called all the leaders of Israel to meet him at Gibeon, where the old wilderness tabernacle was still standing. The ark was not there any more, for David had moved it for safekeeping into Jerusalem; but the brasen altar made by Bezaleel was still in its old place outside the faded tent, and Solomon offered a thousand burnt offerings upon it as a mark of his devotion to God.

The fact that he, the new young king, was starting his reign in this way must have made a great impression on everybody who was there. Quickly the story spread all over the country, bringing hope of a great revival.

One night while Solomon was in Gibeon, the Lord appeared to him in a dream and asked, "What shall I give thee?"

Solomon answered, "Thou hast shewed unto thy servant David my father great mercy, according as he walked before thee in truth, and in righteousness, and in uprightness of heart with thee; and thou hast kept for him this great kindness, that thou hast given him a son to sit on his throne, as it is this day.

"And now, O Lord my God, thou hast made thy servant king instead of David my father: and I am but a little child: I know not how to go out or come in. And thy servant is in the midst of thy people which thou hast chosen, a great people, that cannot be numbered nor counted for multitude.

"Give therefore thy servant an understanding heart to judge thy people, that I may discern between good and bad: for who is able to judge this thy so great a people?"

God was much pleased with Solomon's prayer. What a noble petition it was. Many a young man would have asked for a nice new chariot, or a gold-plated suit of armor, or maybe some fine Arabian horses, but not this youth.

SOLOMON'S PRAYER FOR WISDOM

Instead he merely asked for wisdom to do his job as it should be done.

And God said to him, "Because thou hast asked this thing, and hast not asked for thyself long life; neither hast asked riches for thyself, nor hast asked the life of thine enemies; but hast asked for thyself understanding to discern judgment; behold, I have done according to thy words: lo, I have given thee a wise and an understanding heart; . . . and I have also given thee that which thou hast not asked, both riches, and honour: so that there shall not be any among the kings like unto thee all thy days. And if thou wilt walk in my ways, to keep my statutes and my commandments, as thy father David did walk, then I will lengthen thy days."

"And Solomon awoke; and, behold, it was a dream."

But what a beautiful dream! And what a lesson it has for every boy and girl today!

If God should say to you, What shall I give thee? what would you say to Him? Would you ask for the latest model car? Or for a beautiful, expensive home? Or for lots of money? Or that you might be at the top of your class? Or that you might win first prize at your school games?

Or would you say, like Solomon, "Just make me wise, dear Lord, so that I may always choose the right, and so please Thee in all things"?

If you will pray a prayer like this, asking only for wisdom to do God's will, it will please Him very much indeed. And He will answer you as surely as He did King Solomon, giving you not only wisdom but everything else you need.

133

As newly appointed ruler of the kingdom Solomon felt his responsibility so much that he asked God not for fame or wealth or power, but only for wisdom to rule his people.

STORY 4

Dividing a Baby

ONE OF the first problems the new king met was a very difficult one. Two women came to him, both claiming the same baby. They wanted him to decide whose it was. But how could he tell?

Sitting on his throne, Solomon listened carefully to their story.

The two women lived together in the same house. Their babies had been born about the same time, one three days before the other. Then one of the babies had died.

Said the first woman, "O my lord, . . . this woman's child died in the night; because she overlaid it. And she arose at midnight, and took my son from beside me, while thine hand-maid slept, and laid it in her bosom, and laid her dead child in my bosom."

When she awoke in the morning to feed her baby, so she said, she found a dead child in her arms which was not hers, but the other woman's.

134

DIVIDING A BABY

"No!" cried the other woman frantically, "but the living is my son, and the dead is thy son!"

"No!" yelled the first woman, "but the dead is thy son, and the living is my son!"

What a scene that must have been in the palace, with these two angry women shouting at each other, ready to tear out each other's hair if they had the chance!

Poor Solomon! He had never met anything like this before. If ever he needed the wisdom which God had promised him, it was now.

"Bring me a sword," he said calmly, and a servant brought him one, while silence fell in the room.

"Whatever is he going to do with that sword?" someone whispered.

"Now the baby!" said the king.

There was a gasp. Surely he was not going to cut the baby in half!

"Divide the living child in two," said Solomon, "and give half to the one and half to the other."

Everybody was shocked.

"No! Please don't!" screamed the real mother. "O my lord, give her the living child, and in no wise slay it."

"No," said the other woman heartlessly, "let it be neither mine nor thine, but divide it."

"Aha!" mused Solomon; "now I know to whom the child belongs." Then, pointing to the woman who had asked that the baby's life be spared, he said, "Give her the living child, and in no wise slay it: she is the mother thereof."

As the two women went out from the presence of the king their story went with them. It leaped from city to city and from village to village till everybody from one end of the country to the other was talking about that baby, and how Solomon had found out who its mother was.

"And all Israel heard of the judgment which the king had judged; and they feared the king: for they saw that the wisdom of God was in him to do judgment."

≈≈≈≈≈≈≈

STORY 5

Israel's Happiest Days

≈≈≈≈≈≈≈≈≈≈≈

UNDER King Solomon the children of Israel enjoyed their happiest days. Never had they been so rich. Never had they known such peace.

"Judah and Israel were many, as the sand which is by the sea in multitude, eating and drinking, and making merry."

Those were good times indeed!

"And Solomon reigned over all the kingdoms from the river [Euphrates] unto the land of the Philistines, and unto the border of Egypt: they brought presents, and served Solomon all the days of his life. . . . He had peace on all sides round about him. And Judah and Israel dwelt safely, every man under his vine and under his fig tree, from Dan even to Beer-sheba, all the days of Solomon."

With no enemies to fear and no wars to fight, Solomon was able to devote himself almost entirely to the task of building the temple his father had planned and prepared for so lovingly.

137

Though David had made great preparations, and gathered much lumber, and metals of various kinds, they were not enough. As Solomon looked over the plans for the temple his father had given him, he saw that he would need much more material before he could start to build.

So he sent to David's old friend Hiram, king of Tyre, and asked him for help. In particular he wanted more cedar and fir trees out of the forests of Lebanon. He offered to pay well for them and to send men to help cut them, "for," he said graciously, "thou knowest that there is not among us any that can . . . hew timber like unto the Sidonians."

King Hiram was equally courteous and sent back a message, saying, "Blessed be the Lord this day, which hath given unto David a wise son over this great people." Then he promised to do everything Solomon asked.

"I will do all thy desire concerning timber of cedar, and concerning timber of fir," he wrote. "My servants shall bring them down from Lebanon unto the sea: and I will convey them by sea in floats unto the place that thou shalt appoint me, . . . and thou shalt receive them."

So more and more trees were felled and floated down the coast as far as Joppa. Then Solomon's men hauled them up the steep road to Jerusalem. It was a long and heavy task and took years to complete.

"So Hiram gave Solomon cedar trees and fir trees according to all his desire. And Solomon gave Hiram twenty thousand measures of wheat for food to his household, and twenty

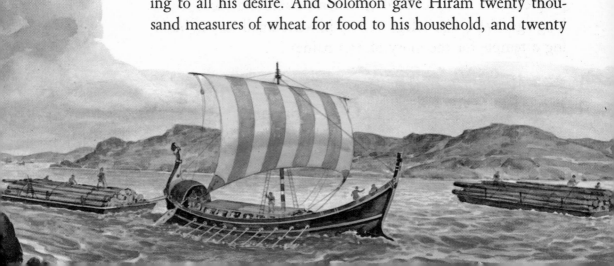

measures of pure oil: thus gave Solomon to Hiram year by year."

To help Hiram in the cutting and sawing, Solomon called for thirty thousand men, sending ten thousand every month to Lebanon in rotation. In addition he had seventy thousand men helping in other ways, and eighty thousand "hewers in the mountains."

At the king's command these men brought "great stones, costly stones, and hewed stones, to lay the foundations of the house. And Solomon's builders and Hiram's builders did hew them, and the stonesquarers: so they prepared timber and stones to build the house."

What excitement there must have been as the piles of lumber and hewn stones grew greater and greater! For by this time the building of the temple had become the center of interest for all Israel. With so many thousands at work on the project, and so many more thousands busy feeding them, it must have been the main topic of conversation from one end of the country to the other.

Nobody minded the work. It was so much better than fighting the Philistines, the Amalekites, the Ammonites, and the rest of their enemies, as they had had to do for so many weary, discouraging years.

A great new day had dawned for Israel.

Peace! How wonderful it was! God was blessing His people as He had promised Abraham, Isaac, and Jacob in the long ago. What a privilege to help in some small way in building a temple for the glory of His name!

139

STORY 6

Huram, the Brass Caster

O NE OF the special requests that Solomon made of King Hiram of Tyre was for a man skilled in handling metals.

"Send me now therefore a man cunning to work in gold, in silver, and in brass, and in iron," he wrote to his friend.

What he needed was another Bezaleel, who did such wonderful work in the building of the wilderness tabernacle and its furniture. And King Hiram found such a man. His name was Huram, a citizen of Tyre, whose mother belonged to the tribe of Dan. Strangely, he was distantly related, through his mother, to Aholiab, who had been Bezaleel's right-hand helper nearly five hundred years before.

This young man, just like Bezaleel and Aholiab, was "filled with wisdom, and understanding," and "skilful to work in gold, and in silver, in brass, in iron, in stone, and in timber, in purple, in blue, and in fine linen, and in crimson, also to grave any manner of graving." A wonder boy indeed! And

140

a trouble shooter, too, for King Hiram said of him that he could "find out every device which shall be put to him."

The king's description was not overdrawn—not when you know what young Huram did.

When he arrived in Jerusalem and looked over the plans of the temple, he saw that his biggest job was to cast two great pillars of brass, or bronze, that were to stand in front of it.

These pillars were to be thirty-three feet high (18 cubits) and over seven feet thick. Where could such massive pillars be cast? Where could enough clay be found to make the molds for them?

It was a problem that would have stumped most people, but not Huram. He looked around until he found the clay— away down in the Jordan valley "between Succoth and Zarthan."

Then he must have asked himself, "Shall I take the metal to the clay or bring the clay to the metal?" Either way meant an immense amount of work.

He decided to cast the pillars in the valley. So he set up his furnaces down there, melted the metal, then poured it into the molds he had fashioned in the clay ground.

Finally, when all was done, he produced two magnificent pillars of gleaming bronze.

But now he had to get them up the mountain to Jerusalem. How did he do it? Nobody knows for sure. The pillars were long and heavy and the mountain trail steep and winding, with many a hairpin bend. But there was no stopping Huram. Somehow or other he got those two pillars up to

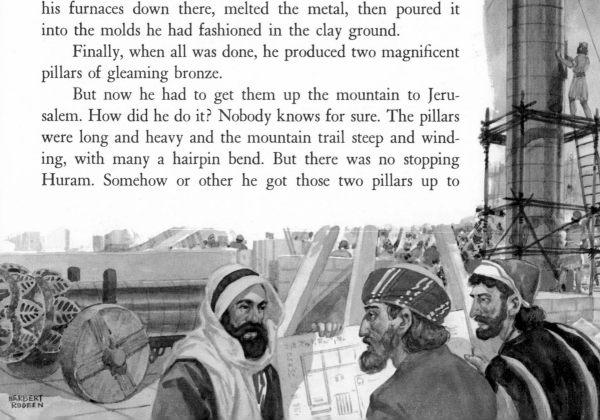

Jerusalem and put them in place before the temple. Known as "Jachin" (meaning, "He shall establish"), and "Boaz" (meaning, "In it is strength"), they stood for hundreds of years to the glory of God and as a reminder of what a man can do when he puts his mind to his work.

While Huram's laborers were still working on the pillars and dragging them inch by inch up the mountainside, he was busy making many other things, some of them almost as big and important as the two great pillars. For instance, he made a great bronze bowl or "molten sea," eighteen feet in diameter and over nine feet deep. This stood upon twelve bronze oxen, "three looking toward the north, and three looking toward the west, and three looking toward the south, and three looking toward the east."

This was no easy task, for the huge bowl was made of metal "a hand breadth thick, and the brim thereof was wrought like the brim of a cup, with flowers of lilies: it contained two thousand baths." In today's measurements that would be almost twelve thousand gallons.

Some of the other things Huram made are listed in the record: "four hundred pomegranates" and "ten bases, and ten lavers on the bases; and . . . the pots, and the shovels, and the basons," all of "bright brass," that is, burnished bronze.

This man helped in many other ways in the building of the temple, and when we speak of that beautiful house of God as Solomon's Temple we should not forget all the labor of love which Huram and thousands of other people put into it.

STORY 7

Building in Silence

I T TOOK Solomon four years to gather all the material needed for the building of the temple, and seven more years to put it together.

One reason why the preparations took so long was that every stone and every piece of metal or wood was cut to size, or molded to shape, before it was brought to the building site. As a result not a sound was to be heard while the temple was taking shape. "There was neither hammer nor axe nor any tool of iron heard in the house, while it was in building."

Just as silently as God works in nature, causing the grass to grow and the trees to bud, blossom, and bear fruit without a sound, so noiselessly was His temple built.

Perhaps God intended it to be a lesson to His people to remind them how He plans to build His church on earth—not by loud, noisy methods, but by the quiet working of His Holy Spirit upon the hearts of men and women. Some boys and girls should remember this when they go to church!

143

As stone was laid on stone, each fitting perfectly in its appointed place, the building gradually took shape. No doubt many fathers and mothers from Jerusalem and nearby villages brought their children to see the great sight and gaze in wonder as the silent builders worked. For years—long before David's death—they had heard stories about this glorious temple; now it was growing before their eyes. And from the huge size of the blocks of stone being used for the foundations, they could see it was going to be even more wonderful than they had dreamed.

In size the temple was just twice as large as the tabernacle Moses built in the wilderness.

Moses' tabernacle was 30 cubits long (55 feet) and Solomon's Temple, 60 cubits (110 feet).

Moses' tabernacle was 10 cubits wide (18 feet) and Solomon's Temple, 20 cubits wide (36 feet).

Moses' tabernacle was 10 cubits high (18 feet) and Solomon's Temple, 20 cubits high (36 feet).

Just as the wilderness tabernacle had been divided into two parts, the holy place and the most holy place, or holy of holies, so was the temple.

All the walls and ceiling were lined with cedar, and the floor with "planks of fir," so that there was "no stone seen." Then all the wood was covered with gold. Solomon "overlaid also the house, the beams, the posts, and the walls thereof, and the doors thereof, with gold; and graved cherubims on the walls. . . . And he made the vail of blue, and purple, and crimson, and fine linen, and wrought cherubims thereon."

144

BUILDING IN SILENCE

Within the holy of holies he placed two cherubim carved from olive wood, also overlaid with gold, whose wings touched the walls on either side.

In the holy place he put a new golden altar of incense, new golden tables for the shewbread, and ten golden candlesticks, five on the right side and five on the left.

How beautiful it must have been inside, with the bright colors of the veil, or curtain, and the twinkling lights of the ten candlesticks, all reflected in the polished gold of the walls, floor, and ceiling!

Outside the temple a great bronze altar, thirty-six feet square and eighteen feet high, was built for the offering of sacrifices.

At the southeast corner was the "molten sea" made by Huram, which was really a bathing pool for the priests. Besides this there were ten bronze lavers, or wash places, for cleansing the sacrifices before they were offered.

At last, seven years after the work was started, the building was finished. The plans that God had given to David had been carried out to the letter. Everything, from the laying of the foundation stones to the polishing of the last bronze pomegranate, had been done as well as men could do it. Everyone, from Solomon to the humblest stonecutter, had done his best to make this the most glorious temple ever built.

Now all that remained was the dedication. Would God accept this building as His own and honor it with His presence as He had honored the tabernacle in the wilderness?

STORY 8

The Temple Dedicated

ONE THING was missing from the temple.

The golden candlesticks were in place, also the golden tables for the shewbread, the golden altar of incense, the many-colored curtains, and the two golden cherubim, but—there was no ark. This was still in the tent which David had made for it when he had brought it from Kirjath-jearim to Jerusalem.

So when all the work on the temple was done and everything had been made as perfect as possible, Solomon "assembled the elders of Israel, and all the heads of the tribes, the chief of the fathers of the children of Israel, unto Jerusalem, to bring up the ark of the covenant of the Lord out of the city of David, which is Zion."

What a procession that must have been! And what joy must have filled every heart as the people saw the precious ark —now nearly five hundred years old—carried reverently by the Levites to what they all believed would be its final rest-

146

ing place in the holy of holies of the beautiful new temple!

At the same time the priests and Levites brought all that was left of the old tabernacle, with "all the holy vessels" that were in it, and stored them carefully in the new building.

As the priests "brought in the ark of the covenant of the Lord unto his place, . . . even under the wings of the cherubims," they must have noticed how small it seemed. For it was only 55 inches long and 33 inches wide, while the new holy of holies was 36 feet square and 36 feet high, and each of the cherubim was 18 feet from wing tip to wing tip.

Yet, though the ark was so small and had nothing in it "save the two tables which Moses put therein at Horeb," it was the most precious and important thing in the temple. Without it—without the law of God inside it and the mercy seat above it—the services in the temple would have been meaningless.

Suddenly, as the priests came out of the temple, having left the ark in place, there was a great burst of music and song. A hundred and twenty priests blew trumpets, while scores of Levites began to play on cymbals, harps, and psalteries, while others started to sing the praises of God.

Then "as the trumpeters and singers were as one, to make one sound to be heard in praising and thanking the Lord; and when they lifted up their voice with the trumpets and

cymbals and instruments of musick, and praised the Lord, saying, For he is good; for his mercy endureth for ever: . . . the house was filled with a cloud, even the house of the Lord."

Solomon, standing on a bronze platform five feet high in the midst of the court before the temple, was told what had happened, and knew that "the glory of the Lord had filled the house of God."

Deeply moved that God had been pleased to show this mark of approval, he "spread forth his hands toward heaven" before the thousands of people crowded around him, and prayed a most beautiful prayer of dedication.

"O Lord God of Israel," he cried, "there is no God like thee in the heaven, nor in the earth; which keepest covenant, and shewest mercy unto thy servants, that walk before thee with all their hearts. . . . But will God in very deed dwell with men on the earth? behold, heaven and the heaven of heavens cannot contain thee; how much less this house which I have built!

"Have respect therefore to the prayer of thy servant, and to his supplication, O Lord my God, to hearken unto the cry and the prayer which thy servant prayeth before thee: that thine eyes may be open upon this house day and night, upon the place whereof thou hast said that thou wouldest put thy

148

name there; to hearken unto the prayer which thy servant prayeth toward this place.

"Hearken therefore unto the supplications of thy servant, and of thy people Israel, which they shall make toward this place: hear thou from thy dwelling place, even from heaven; and when thou hearest, forgive."

Then the king made seven special requests of God:

1. "If a man sin against his neighbour" and the matter be brought to the temple, then, he asked, "hear thou from heaven, and do, and judge thy servants."

2. "If thy people Israel be put to the worse before the enemy, because they have sinned against thee; and shall return and confess thy name, and pray and make supplication before thee in this house; then hear thou from the heavens, and forgive the sin of thy people."

3. In time of drought, when there is no rain, he said, "if they pray toward this place, and confess thy name, and turn from their sin, . . . then hear thou from heaven and forgive the sin of thy servants, . . . and send rain upon thy land."

4. "If there be dearth in the land, if there be pestilence, if there be . . . mildew, locusts, or caterpillars . . . whatsoever sore or whatsoever sickness there be: then what prayer or what supplication soever shall be made of any man, . . . when every one shall know his own sore and his own grief, and shall spread forth his hands toward this house: then hear thou from heaven thy dwelling place, and forgive."

5. If a stranger should come from a far country and pray in this house, he pleaded, then, "hear thou from the heavens,

even from thy dwelling place, and do according to all that the stranger calleth to thee for; that all people of the earth may know thy name."

6. "If thy people go out to war against their enemies by the way that thou shalt send them, and they pray unto thee toward this city . . . and the house which I have built for thy name; then hear from the heavens their prayer and their supplication, and maintain their cause."

7. "If they sin against thee, (for there is no man which sinneth not,) and thou be angry with them, and deliver them over before their enemies, and they carry them away captives unto a land far off or near. . . . If they return to thee with all their heart and with all their soul in the land of their captivity . . . : then hear thou from the heavens, even from thy dwelling place . . . , and forgive."

Then, as he ended his prayer, he cried, "Now therefore arise, O Lord God, into thy resting place, thou, and the ark of thy strength: let thy priests, O Lord God, be clothed with salvation, and let thy saints rejoice in goodness."

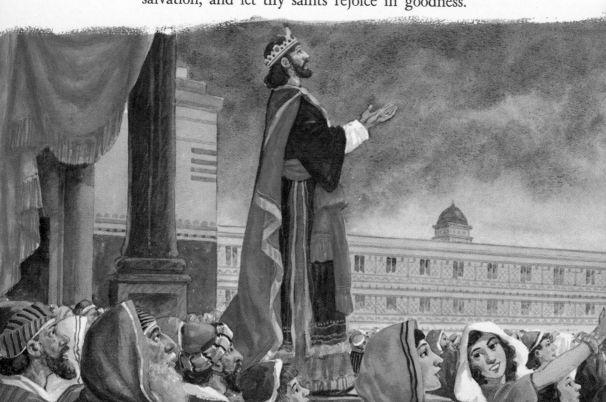

THE TEMPLE DEDICATED

Such a beautiful prayer it was! So full of kindness and thoughtfulness for others! And there is no doubt that God heard it in heaven, His dwelling place. For no sooner had Solomon finished praying than "fire came down from heaven, and consumed the burnt offering and the sacrifices; and the glory of the Lord filled the house."

When all the thousands who had gathered for this great and glorious ceremony saw the fire fall, and how the beautiful new temple was radiant with the glory of the Lord, "they bowed themselves with their faces to the ground upon the pavement, and worshipped, and praised the Lord, saying, For he is good; for his mercy endureth for ever."

And when the mothers put their children to bed that night, I am sure that more than one boy or girl must have said, "Mamma, did you see the fire come down from heaven today? Wasn't it wonderful? How near God must have been just then!"

STORY 9

Words of Warning

AFTER the solemn service of dedication, Solomon held a great feast for all the crowds who had come to Jerusalem. It lasted seven days. Then "on the eighth day he sent the people away: and they blessed the king, and went unto their tents joyful and glad of heart for all the goodness that the Lord had done for David his servant, and for Israel his people."

When they had all gone home and things had begun to settle down again, "the Lord appeared to Solomon the second time."

The first time was at Gibeon, just after his coronation, when he prayed that lovely prayer for wisdom and God granted his request.

Now the Lord had something more to say to him.

"I have heard thy prayer and thy supplication, that thou hast made before me," He said, referring to his prayer at the dedication of the temple. "I have hallowed this house, which

152

thou hast built, to put my name there for ever; . . . and if thou wilt walk before me, as David thy father walked, in integrity of heart, and in uprightness, to do according to all that I have commanded thee, . . . then I will establish the throne of thy kingdom upon Israel for ever. . . .

"But"—and at this Solomon must have listened with some anxiety—"if ye shall at all turn from following me, ye or your children, and will not keep my commandments and my statutes which I have set before you, but go and serve other gods, and worship them: then will I cut off Israel out of the land which I have given them; and this house, which I have hallowed for my name, will I cast out of my sight; and Israel shall be a proverb and a byword among all people: and at this house, which is high, every one that passeth by it shall be astonished, and shall hiss; and they shall say, Why hath the Lord done thus unto this land, and to this house?

"And they shall answer, Because they forsook the Lord their God."

This house, this glorious temple, cast out of God's sight! How could that ever be? thought Solomon. Impossible! Surely God would never let anything so beautiful, so solidly built, be destroyed!

Strange words they were indeed for God to use about a building on which the young king had spent seven of the

best years of his life. Was there need of this solemn warning?

There was indeed, as we shall see.

Already Solomon had married the daughter of the king of Egypt, and there was always the danger that her children might want to worship the heathen gods she once served.

Already he was fast becoming the richest man in the world, with more gold and silver pouring into Jerusalem than its people had ever seen before.

Already he was beginning to spend money lavishly and to live in luxury, with all the perils which that sort of life always brings.

So God warned him to be careful how he lived from now on; that obedience to His commandments is more important in His sight than all the beautiful buildings ever built.

Doing God's will, speaking the truth, thinking pure thoughts, living a godly life—these mean far more to Him than the best and biggest things any of us can build of stone, or wood, or gold, or silver.

Oh, yes, God was willing that the temple Solomon had built should stand forever. He said so. But only if Solomon and his children would be true to Him always. If they should forsake Him, and follow other gods, then it would disappear from the face of the earth. No matter how firm its foundations, how massive its walls, how costly its golden ornaments, it would be carried away like chaff before the wind.

And the only reason why Solomon's Temple is not to be found in Jerusalem today is because God's word came true. His warning was forgotten and the temple vanished.

STORY 10

The Queen of Sheba

A S NEWS of Solomon's wealth and wisdom spread abroad, more and more kings and rulers came to visit him. "All the earth sought to Solomon, to hear his wisdom, which God had put in his heart. And they brought every man his present, vessels of silver, and vessels of gold, and garments, and armour, and spices, horses, and mules, a rate year by year."

"All the kings of Arabia and governors of the country brought gold and silver to Solomon." And as each visitor brought some rich present, Solomon grew richer and richer.

The gold that came to him in one year weighed 666 talents —a very large sum of money—besides what came to him from "the merchantmen, and . . . the traffick of the spice merchants."

To increase his wealth still further he built two fleets, one on the Red Sea to bring gold from the land of Ophir, and one on the Mediterranean Sea to trade with lands to the west. "Once in three years" these ships came home, "bringing gold, and silver, ivory, and apes, and peacocks." He had one thou-

sand four hundred chariots and twelve thousand horsemen, and he made silver as common as stones in Jerusalem.

With some of his wealth Solomon built "a great throne of ivory, and overlaid it with the best gold." This throne had six steps, with lions on either side of each step and two more on either side of the throne itself, making fourteen lions in all. No wonder the Bible says "there was not the like made in any kingdom." It must have made quite an impression on visitors.

"And all king Solomon's drinking vessels were of gold, . . . none were of silver: it was nothing accounted of in the days of Solomon."

Among the many famous people who came to see Solomon was the Queen of Sheba. She lived, many believe, in the southern part of Arabia, and her journey to Jerusalem was a long and tiring one, for she came "with a very great train, with camels that bare spices, and very much gold, and precious stones."

She must have been a very wise woman herself, for she was eager for more knowledge, and having heard of the fame of Solomon, "came to prove him with hard questions." The Bible does not tell us what her questions were about, only that Solomon answered them all and so made her very happy.

No doubt she, too, walked up the six steps of the magnificent gold and ivory throne, between the twelve lions, for when she had seen "all Solomon's wisdom, and the house that he had built, and the meat of his table, and the sitting of his servants, and the attendance of his ministers, and their ap-

157

Accompanied by a long column of servants, horses, and camels carrying spices, gold, precious stones, and other riches of her kingdom, the Queen of Sheba came to visit Solomon.

parel, and his cupbearers, and his ascent by which he went up unto the house of the Lord; there was no more spirit in her."

"It was a true report that I heard in mine own land of thy acts and of thy wisdom," she said to the king. "Howbeit I believed not the words, until I came, and mine eyes had seen it: and, behold, the half was not told me: thy wisdom and prosperity exceedeth the fame which I heard. Happy are thy men, happy are these thy servants, which stand continually before thee, and that hear thy wisdom."

Then she added this word of praise to Solomon's God, giving Him the glory for all that she had seen and heard: "Blessed be the Lord thy God, which delighteth in thee, to set thee on the throne of Israel: because the Lord loved Israel for ever, therefore made he thee king, to do judgment and justice."

Then she gave Solomon 120 talents of gold and "of spices very great store, and precious stones: there came no more such abundance of spices as these which the Queen of Sheba gave to king Solomon."

As she returned to her own country the queen took away with her the wonderful memory of a king whom the God of heaven had greatly prospered, and of a land richly blessed.

If only Solomon had continued to witness for his God like this, how much good he might have done! How many kings and queens might have learned of God's goodness and love! With his wealth and wisdom Solomon could have filled the world with the knowledge of the Lord. Alas, he did not do so. The world's wisest man was one of God's worst disappointments.

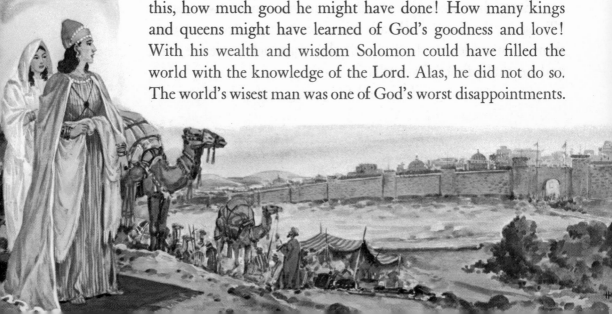

STORY 11

Wisdom of the Wise

D AY BY DAY, year after year, there flowed from
Solomon's bright, keen mind a river of wisdom. "He
spake three thousand proverbs: and his songs were
a thousand and five."

No doubt he had a "scribe," or secretary, to write down
his wise sayings as he thought of them. Many are to be found
in the books of Proverbs and Ecclesiastes.

Here is some of his good advice for students:

"If thou criest after knowledge, and liftest up thy voice
for understanding; if thou seekest her as silver, and searchest
for her as for hid treasures; then shalt thou understand the
fear of the Lord, and find the knowledge of God."

Every boy and girl should memorize these two verses:
"Trust in the Lord with all thine heart; and lean not unto
thine own understanding. In all thy ways acknowledge him,
and he shall direct thy paths."

Here is more good counsel for young and old: "Enter not

into the path of the wicked, and go not in the way of evil men. Avoid it, pass not by it, turn from it and pass away. . . . But the path of the just is as the shining light, that shineth more and more unto the perfect day."

Watching some ants one day, he saw a lesson for lazy people: "Go to the ant, thou sluggard; consider her ways, and be wise: which having no guide, overseer, or ruler, provideth her meat in the summer, and gathereth her food in the harvest. . . . Yet a little sleep, a little slumber, a little folding of the hands to sleep; so shall thy poverty come as one that travelleth, and thy want as an armed man."

About the use of wine and all drinks that have alcohol in them, he had some very wise things to say: "Wine is a mocker, strong drink is raging: and whosoever is deceived thereby is not wise."

"Who hath woe? who hath sorrow? who hath contentions? who hath babbling? who hath wounds without cause? who hath redness of eyes? They that tarry long at the wine; they that go to seek mixed wine. Look not thou upon the wine when it is red. . . . At the last it biteth like a serpent, and stingeth like an adder."

Here are more precious gems of wisdom, on all sorts of subjects:

"A talebearer revealeth secrets: but he that is of a faithful spirit concealeth the matter."

"The liberal soul shall be made fat."

"He that winneth souls is wise."

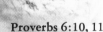

Proverbs 4:18

Proverbs 6:10, 11

Proverbs 11:13

Proverbs 20:1

WISDOM OF THE WISE

"Lying lips are abomination to the Lord: but they that deal truly are his delight."

"A soft answer turneth away wrath: but grievous words stir up anger."

Proverbs 15:1

"Pride goeth before destruction, and an haughty spirit before a fall."

"He that is slow to anger is better than the mighty."

"A friend loveth at all times, and a brother is born for adversity."

"A merry heart doeth good like a medicine."

"A man that hath friends must show himself friendly: and there is a friend that sticketh closer than a brother."

Proverbs 17:22

"Even a child is known by his doings, whether his work be pure, and whether it be right."

"A good name is rather to be chosen than great riches, and loving favour rather than silver and gold."

"Train up a child in the way he should go: and when he is old, he will not depart from it."

"A word fitly spoken is like apples of gold in pictures of silver."

"Faithful are the wounds of a friend."

"He that covereth his sins shall not prosper: but whoso confesseth and forsaketh them shall have mercy."

Proverbs 22:6

It would be good for you to memorize all these proverbs. Certainly anyone who tries to follow their good advice will live a happy, prosperous life. For this is not merely the wisdom of Solomon: it is also the wisdom of God.

Proverbs 22:1

Proverbs 28:13

STORY 12

One Big "But"

GREAT, wise, and rich though he was, Solomon had one big "but" in his life. You will find it in the first verse of the eleventh chapter of the first book of Kings.

"*But* king Solomon loved many strange women."

He had many, many wives. Hundreds of them. So many, in fact, that he could hardly have remembered all their names.

The worst of it was that these women were not Israelites, but "Moabites, Ammonites, Edomites, Zidonians, and Hittites," the very women whom God had expressly forbidden His people to marry.

No doubt one reason why Solomon married so many wives was that each one brought with her a big dowry from a wealthy father. But though his wives brought him great riches, they "turned away his heart."

As a young man he began his reign with his heart set on God. That is why he built the temple and prayed that wonderful prayer of dedication.

162

But when the foreign princesses came flocking into Jerusalem, they wanted to worship their own gods. Of course. They did not know any better. Some were followers of Ashtoreth, the goddess of the Zidonians, others of Molech, "the abomination of the Ammonites." To please them, and keep them happy and peaceful, Solomon built places of worship for these heathen gods.

"Likewise did he for all his strange wives, which burnt incense and sacrificed unto their gods."

The good people of Jerusalem must have been shocked. To think that their king, the son of David, should permit such idolatry within sight of the beautiful temple! It was awful!

The worship of Molech called for the sacrifice of living children, who were made to "pass through the fire," screaming in pain and fright. How could Solomon, who had shown such tenderness toward a baby when the two women came to him, now permit such horrible torture of innocent little ones? How far could a man fall?

No wonder "the Lord was angry with Solomon."

He had reason to be. Twice He had appeared to the king in his younger days with promises of great blessing if he would

do right and follow the ways of God. Now Solomon had failed Him. With all the wisdom the Lord had given him, he had allowed himself to become a fool. "He kept not that which the Lord commanded," and soon began to pay the price of his disobedience and folly.

"Wherefore the Lord said unto Solomon, Forasmuch as this is done of thee, and thou hast not kept my covenant and my statutes, which I have commanded thee, I will surely rend the kingdom from thee."

How sad! How terribly sad!

He had started out so well, and God had blessed him so greatly! Now he was rejected, like Saul before him.

He had gained riches, power, prestige, everything a man could wish for, but he had forgotten God. And in losing God he had lost all.

Is there a "but" in your life? Could it be said of you, This boy has a nice home, many fine toys, a new bicycle, *BUT* he tells lies, or he can't be trusted, or he hates going to church?

Or, This girl has wonderful parents, beautiful clothes, the best of everything, *BUT* she is cross, grumbly, impatient, and never says her prayers?

Let's beware of the "buts" in our lives.

164

PART IV

Stories of Solomon

(1 KINGS 12:1-16:34)

STORY 1

Price of Folly

WHAT a price there was to pay for Solomon's fool-ishness!

Those foreign princesses he invited into his palace not only brought their idols and their false religions with them; they brought a lot of trouble, too.

When the people of Israel saw their great and famous king allowing such things to happen in Jerusalem, some of them naturally began to think that the gods of the heathen couldn't be so bad after all. If Solomon the wise thought they were all right, what could be wrong with them? So idolatry began to spread through the land, and took such hold that for hundreds of years nobody was able to get rid of it.

As the people slowly turned from God, so He turned from them. His blessings were withdrawn, and darkness fell, even as when the sun goes behind a cloud.

Whereas for a little while the kingdom of Israel had been at peace, from the river Euphrates to the border of Egypt,

167

← PAINTING BY VERNON NYE   © 1955, BY REVIEW AND HERALD

The prophet Ahijah took off his beautiful new garment, tore it into twelve pieces, and gave ten of them to Jeroboam to show that God had made him ruler over the ten tribes of Israel.

now revolutions began to break out, first in one place, then in another. One was led by Hadad the Edomite, another by Rezon, the ruler of Syria, "an adversary to Israel all the days of Solomon." Then Jeroboam, one of Solomon's most trusted servants, turned against him.

One day as this man was walking alone in a field near Jerusalem, the prophet Ahijah met him, wearing a brand-new garment.

To Jeroboam's surprise, Ahijah took off this new garment, tore it into twelve pieces, and gave ten of them to him. Then the prophet said, "Take thee ten pieces: for thus saith the Lord, the God of Israel, Behold, I will rend the kingdom out of the hand of Solomon, and will give ten tribes to thee: . . . because they have forsaken me, and have worshipped Ashtoreth the goddess of the Zidonians, Chemosh the god of the Moabites, and Milcom [Molech] the god of the children of Ammon, and have not walked in my ways, to do that which is right in mine eyes, and to keep my statutes and my judgments, as did David his father. . . . And I will take thee, and thou . . . shalt be king over Israel."

This is something to think about. Solomon had all those wives and, no doubt, many children, but God passed them all by and gave ten of the twelve tribes to a servant! So great must have been His displeasure at the way Solomon had failed Him!

When Solomon heard that Ahijah had told Jeroboam the Lord had chosen him to be king, he sought to kill him. "And Jeroboam arose, and fled into Egypt, unto Shishak king

of Egypt, and was in Egypt until the death of Solomon."

As the aging king saw his friends deserting him, and all the trouble his wives had brought him, he came to see what a dreadful failure he had made of everything.

Looking back over his life he said:

"I made me great works; I builded me houses; I planted me vineyards: I made me gardens and orchards, and I planted trees in them of all kind of fruits: I made me pools of water, to water therewith the wood that bringeth forth trees: I got me servants and maidens, and had servants born in my house; also I had great possessions of great and small cattle above all that were in Jerusalem before me: I gathered me also silver

169

and gold, and the peculiar treasure of kings and of the provinces:
I gat me men singers and women singers, and the delights of
the sons of men, as musical instruments, and that of all sorts.

"So I was great, and increased more than all that were
before me in Jerusalem: also my wisdom remained with me.
And whatsoever mine eyes desired I kept not from them, I
withheld not my heart from any joy; for my heart rejoiced
in all my labour: and this was my portion of all my labour.

"Then I looked on all the works that my hands had
wrought, and on the labour that I had laboured to do: and,
behold, all was vanity and vexation of spirit, and there was
no profit under the sun."

No profit! Only vanity! And all because, somewhere
along life's journey, he had left God out.

Toward the end he found God again, and was sorry for
all his mistakes. "Let us hear the conclusion of the whole
matter," he wrote: "Fear God, and keep his commandments:
for this is the whole duty of man. For God shall bring every
work into judgment, with every secret thing, whether it be
good, or whether it be evil."

But then it was too late to put things right, or stop the
consequences of his misdeeds.

What a pity he did not follow this good counsel all his
life! How different everything would have been for him
and for Israel!

STORY 2

The Kingdom Divided

WHEN Solomon died he was buried in the city of David, "and Rehoboam his son reigned in his stead."

The coronation of the new king was planned to take place in Shechem, where there was plenty of room for thousands of people to gather for the great event. "All Israel" went there to make him king.

Meanwhile news of Solomon's death had reached Jeroboam in Egypt, and he, remembering what the prophet Ahijah had said to him, hurried northward to see what would happen next.

When he arrived at Shechem everybody recognized him, for he had been one of Solomon's best-known and most efficient officers before he fled to the court of Pharaoh. Many must have wondered why he had come back so soon after the old king's death. Few suspected that he would soon be the leader of a great rebellion.

After the coronation Jeroboam went, with some of the

171

leaders of Israel, to the new king and begged him to ease the burdens which Solomon had laid upon the people. They wanted taxes reduced and the compulsory service laws abolished—for Solomon, in his great building program, had taxed the people heavily and compelled tens of thousands of people to work for him, whether they wanted to or not.

Rehoboam said he would let them know in three days. Then he talked the matter over with his older counselors, and they advised him to do what the leaders wanted.

"If thou be kind to this people, and please them, and speak good words to them," they said, "they will be thy servants for ever."

Not too sure of himself, Rehoboam turned to the younger men around him and asked what they thought he should do. They told him, in effect, to let the people see "who's boss," and rule with a heavy hand, right from the start.

Foolishly, "he forsook the counsel which the old men gave him," and answered the leaders of Israel "after the advice of the young men, saying, My father made your yoke heavy, but I will add thereto: my father chastised you with whips, but I will chastise you with scorpions."

No wonder there was trouble!

As this report spread among the thousands gathered in Shechem, everybody became very angry. They had come to the coronation hoping for relief, not for

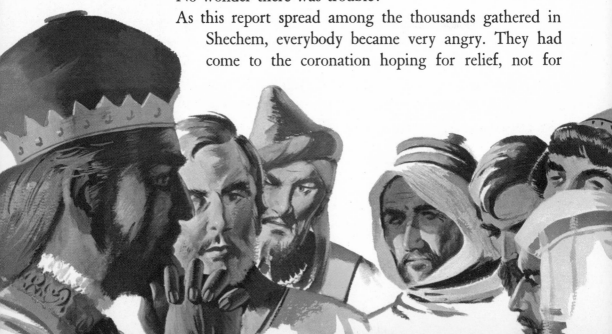

heavier burdens. They had put up with a lot from Solomon, but they were not going to take it from this young upstart.

Suddenly the spirit of revolt flashed from heart to heart, spreading like wildfire through the camp.

"What portion have we in David?" cried the men from the northern tribes. "And we have none inheritance in the son of Jesse: every man to your tents, O Israel: and now, David, see to thine own house. So all Israel went to their tents."

The great rebellion was on.

Ten tribes followed Jeroboam and made him their king. Rehoboam was left with only two tribes, Judah and Benjamin.

When Rehoboam got back to Jerusalem he was very much upset. He saw what a dreadful mistake he had made. By his foolish speech he had lost most of his father's kingdom, and he wanted to get it back again. So he called up all his best soldiers, 180,000 men, and prepared to go and compel the rebels to return.

Just then a man of God named Shemaiah brought him this message: "Ye shall not go up, nor fight against your brethren: return every man to his house: for this thing is done of me."

173

To the credit of young Rehoboam, he obeyed the voice of the Lord and told his soldiers to go back home. Then he decided to make the best of things as they were, and fortified many of the cities that remained to him, in case the rebels should try to take them away from him. "And he fortified the strong holds, and put captains in them and store of victual, [food], and of oil and wine. And in every several city he put shields and spears, and made them exceeding strong, having Judah and Benjamin on his side."

Meanwhile Jeroboam was beginning to reveal the kind of man he really was. No sooner was he made king of the ten tribes than he set up two golden calves for the people to worship. The excuse he made was, "It is too much for you to go up to Jerusalem: behold thy gods, O Israel, which brought thee up out of the land of Egypt. And he set the one in Bethel, and the other put he in Dan."

Then he offered sacrifices to these idols and "made priests of the lowest of the people." As for the Levites, he told them they were not needed any more. So they left their homes and made their way to Jerusalem.

Within five years of Solomon's death his proud, rich empire was torn apart, turned to idols, and its glory vanished.

When Solomon married those heathen princesses he never dreamed all this would happen. He thought he was strong enough and wise enough to stand against their false religions. But he wasn't. His wives had won. First they stole his heart, and now his kingdom.

STORY 3

Solomon's Temple Raided

FOR THREE years all went well with Rehoboam. Priests and Levites whose homes had been in land that was now part of the ten-tribe kingdom came flocking into Jerusalem, together with many others who "set their hearts to seek the Lord God of Israel."

Shocked by all that had happened, the people prayed and worshiped as they had not done for a long time; and it seemed for a while as though there might be a real revival. "They strengthened the kingdom of Judah, and made Rehoboam the son of Solomon strong, three years: for three years they walked in the way of David and Solomon."

But that was about the end of it, for Rehoboam had the same weakness as his father: "he desired many wives." And with much the same result.

"And it came to pass, when Rehoboam had established the kingdom, and had strengthened himself, he forsook the law of the Lord, and all Israel with him."

175

For the next two years both king and people drifted farther and farther from God. Then news reached them that Shishak, king of Egypt, was marching against them with an army of sixty thousand horsemen and twelve hundred chariots.

While Solomon was alive nobody had dared to attack the Hebrew nation. Now it had no defense worth talking about. Easily the Egyptians took all the cities Rehoboam had fortified so carefully. Then they marched on Jerusalem.

"Then came Shemaiah the prophet to Rehoboam, and to the princes of Judah, that were gathered together to Jerusalem because of Shishak, and said unto them, Thus saith the Lord, Ye have forsaken me, and therefore have I also left you in the hand of Shishak."

King and princes were startled. They had never thought that God might desert *them,* though they had long since forgotten *Him.* Falling to their knees, they confessed their sins and cried, "The Lord is righteous."

Ever merciful, the Lord said to Shemaiah, "They have humbled themselves: therefore I will not destroy them, but I will grant them some deliverance; and my wrath shall

not be poured out upon Jerusalem by the hand of Shishak."

So the gates of Jerusalem were opened, and Shishak came in. He had heard much about the wealth of Solomon, and now he saw it for himself. Going straight to the beautiful temple, he ransacked the place and "took away the treasures of the house of the Lord, and the treasures of the king's house; he took all: he carried away also the shields of gold which Solomon had made."

Satisfied with all this loot, he did not destroy the temple or the city, but went back home gloating over his good fortune in getting so much so easily.

When Shishak and his men were gone, Rehoboam and the princes of Judah went to the temple to see what the raiders had left. How sad their hearts must have been as they walked around the plundered building that once had been the glory of Israel and the envy of the world!

Rehoboam made shields of brass to replace Solomon's shields of gold. That in itself tells the story of what had happened to the children of Israel—and how poor they had become—because, once more, they had turned away from God.

STORY 4

The Broken Altar

WICKED though Jeroboam was, God had not turned from him altogether.

One day, as he worshiped before the golden calf which he had set up at Bethel, he heard someone shouting, and turned to see who had dared to interrupt him.

Looking around, he saw a man dressed in the garb of a prophet of God. The man was crying, "O altar, altar, thus saith the Lord; Behold, a child shall be born unto the house of David, Josiah by name; and upon thee shall he offer the priests of the high places that burn incense upon thee, and men's bones shall be burnt upon thee."

Jeroboam was annoyed. The man must be mad! How could he know the name of someone yet unborn, or what that person would do to this altar?

Not for a moment did the king realize that he was being given a glimpse into the future—three hundred years hence—when good king Josiah would break down this very altar and

179

← PAINTING BY KREIGH COLLINS   © 1955, BY REVIEW AND HERALD

When Jeroboam heard the prophecy concerning Josiah and threatened to take the prophet's life, his arm became withered, and God destroyed the altar before his very eyes.

stamp it "small to powder." God was speaking, but he did not know it.

Very angry, he wanted to kill the prophet. But the man of God went on.

"This is the sign which the Lord hath spoken," he said, "Behold, the altar shall be rent, and the ashes that are upon it shall be poured out."

This was too much for Jeroboam.

"Lay hold on him!" he cried to his men, at the same time taking his hand off the altar in an attempt to grab the prophet himself.

Suddenly he stopped. There was an awful pain in his arm. It was withered and paralyzed. Then, hearing a rending noise beside him, he saw his brand-new altar breaking in pieces before his eyes, the ashes on it pouring down the cracks.

He was frightened now, and had good reason to be.

"Pray for me!" he cried.

The prophet prayed, and God, in His great mercy, healed Jeroboam, despite all the wrong he had done. "The king's hand was restored . . . and became as it was before."

This was Jeroboam's last chance to repent and change his life. Did he take it? Did he break down his idols and bring the ten tribes back to God? He did not. Instead he led them ever deeper into sin. The Bible says, "After this thing Jeroboam returned not from his evil way."

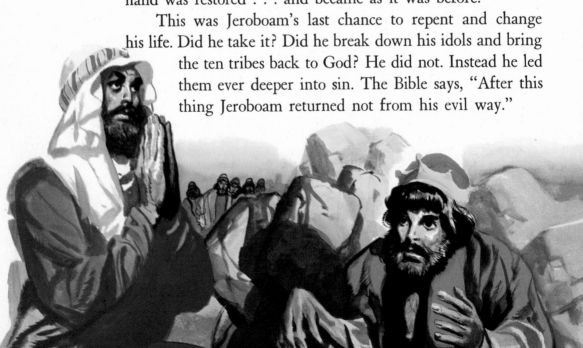

STORY 5

Killed by a Lion

"COME home with me," Jeroboam said to the prophet, "and I will give thee a reward."

"No," said the man of God, "if thou wilt give me half thine house, I will not go in with thee, neither will I eat bread or drink water in this place."

"Why not?" asked Jeroboam.

"Because," he replied, "the Lord said to me, Eat no bread, nor drink water, nor turn again by the same way that thou camest."

So the prophet went back home.

Now it so happened that some boys had seen what had happened to Jeroboam and the altar, and had rushed home to their old father to tell him the news. I can almost hear them saying, "Dad, you should have seen the king's face when he found his arm withered and saw the altar break in pieces!"

"Which way did the prophet go?" the old man asked, anxious to learn more about what had happened.

They told him.

"Saddle my ass," he bade them, and they did.

Then, riding as fast as he could, he hurried after the man of God, finding him at last sitting under an oak.

"Come home with me, and eat bread," he said to him.

"No, thanks," said the man of God, telling him just what he had told Jeroboam.

Then the old man lied to him. "I am a prophet also as thou art," he said; "and an angel spake unto me by the word of the Lord, saying, Bring him back with thee into thine house, that he may eat bread and drink water."

Deceived, the man of God went back with him.

Hardly had he finished his supper, however, than the old man said to him, "Thus saith the Lord, Forasmuch as thou hast disobeyed the mouth of the Lord, and hast not kept the commandment which the Lord thy God commanded thee . . . ; thy carcase shall not come unto the sepulchre of thy fathers."

At once the man of God knew he had made a dreadful mistake. Sadly he got on the ass which the old man gave him, and rode away.

182

KILLED BY A LION

Not far along the road "a lion met him . . . , and slew him." The lion did not eat him, but just left him by the roadside.

Other travelers, passing by, seeing a dead man with a lion and an ass standing beside him, hurried to the city where the old man lived and told their strange story. The old man went out to see if it was true. It was.

There was the lion, the ass, and the body of the man of God. "The lion had not eaten the carcase, nor torn the ass." So the old man put the body on the ass, brought it home, and buried it in his own tomb, saying, "Alas, my brother!"

Such was the fate of the disobedient prophet.

What a lesson for us! How careful we must be! This good man was wonderfully honored by God when he stood before Jeroboam. He saw the altar rent and the king's arm wither. He even saw his prayer for the king answered instantly. Yet twenty-four hours later he was dead, killed by a lion, because he disobeyed God.

STORY 6

Queen in Disguise

S HORTLY after this a great sorrow came to Jeroboam. His son Abijah fell sick, and nobody could do anything for him.

At last Jeroboam remembered the prophet Ahijah, who, years before, had told him that he would someday be king over the ten tribes of Israel. He could make the boy well, if he would. But would he? Not if he knew who the boy really was. That fact must be kept from him at all costs.

So Jeroboam told his wife to disguise herself and go to Shiloh, where Ahijah was living. "Take with thee ten loaves, and cracknels, and a cruse of honey, and go to him: he shall tell thee what shall become of the child."

By this time Ahijah was old and blind, so that there was no need for the queen to disguise herself. But she did, just the same, thinking she could deceive the prophet of the Lord. How mistaken she was! He knew her at once.

To her great amazement, as Ahijah "heard the sound

184

of her feet, as she came in at the door," he said to her, "Come in, thou wife of Jeroboam."

Too startled to speak, the queen never said a word. All she could do was listen to the words of doom the aged prophet spoke to her.

"Go, tell Jeroboam," Ahijah said to her, "Thus saith the Lord God of Israel, Forasmuch as I exalted thee from among the people, and made thee prince over my people Israel, and rent the kingdom away from the house of David, and gave it thee: and yet thou hast not been as my servant David . . . : for thou hast gone and made thee other gods, and molten images, to provoke me to anger, and hast cast me behind thy back: therefore, behold, I will bring evil upon the house of

185

Jeroboam. . . . Him that dieth of Jeroboam in the city shall the dogs eat; and him that dieth in the field shall the fowls of the air eat: for the Lord hath spoken it."

As for Jeroboam's child, there was no hope. He would die; but because God saw "some good thing in him," he only, of all Jeroboam's children, should be buried in a grave.

For the ten tribes which Jeroboam had led into sin, Ahijah had an equally sad message. "The Lord," he said, "shall root up Israel out of this good land, which he gave to their fathers, and shall scatter them beyond the river [Euphrates], because they have made their groves, provoking the Lord to anger."

When Ahijah had finished speaking the queen went sadly on her way, wondering how she would tell her husband what he had said to her.

When she arrived home, at "the threshold of the door," her child died. She knew then that all the other dreadful things Ahijah had told her would come to pass.

You would think that all this would have been enough to turn Jeroboam from his evil ways. But it was not. Like Pharaoh of old, he hardened his heart again, and plunged from one sin into another, till there was no hope for him or for his kingdom.

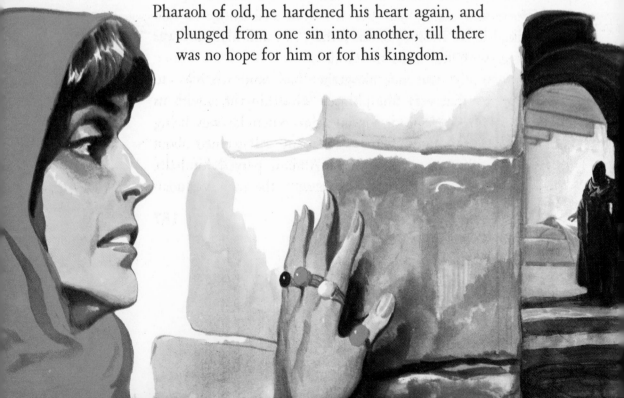

STORY 7

Grandmother's Idol

MEANWHILE, down south, in the kingdom of Judah, King Rehoboam had died. In his place reigned his son Abijam, whose mother, Maachah, had been Rehoboam's favorite wife.

This woman, though a daughter of Absalom and therefore a granddaughter of David, had come under the influence of the heathen religions which Solomon's wives had brought into Jerusalem. She believed in the idols they had set up.

Worse still, she taught her son these evil things so that "he walked in all the sins of his father, . . . and his heart was not perfect with the Lord his God."

However, he was not altogether bad, and we have to thank him for that very fine phrase: "God himself is with us for our captain." He said this one day when he was being attacked by a vast army led by Jeroboam. All seemed about to be lost to the enemy, but when Abijam prayed for help, "the priests sounded with the trumpets," "the men of Judah

187

gave a shout," and defeat was turned into victory.

Soon after that, Abijam died, having reigned only three years. Then Asa came to the throne, and he "did that which was good and right in the eyes of the Lord his God: for he took away the altars of the strange gods, and the high places, and brake down the images."

Just who trained Asa we are not told, but it certainly wasn't his grandmother. She continued to worship her own private idol until one day, when Asa was strong enough, "he removed her from being queen, because she had made an idol in a grove: and Asa cut down her idol, and stamped it, and burnt it at the brook Kidron," just outside Jerusalem.

It must have taken a lot of courage to burn his grandmother's idol, but God was pleased with him for doing it, and blessed him in many ways.

GRANDMOTHER'S IDOL

One day the Ethiopians came up against Judah with one hundred thousand men and three hundred chariots. Asa was alarmed, but he cried to God, saying, "It is nothing with thee to help, whether with many, or with them that have no power: help us, O Lord our God; for we rest on thee, and in thy name we go against this multitude. O Lord, thou art our God; let not man prevail against thee."

In answer to this beautiful prayer God smote the Ethiopians and they fled "and could not recover themselves."

Not long after this King Asa was met by the prophet Azariah, son of Obed, who said to him, "The Lord is with you, while ye be with him; and if ye seek him, he will be found of you; but if ye forsake him, he will forsake you. . . . Be ye strong therefore, and let not your hands be weak: for your work shall be rewarded."

"When Asa heard these words, . . . he took courage," and rid Judah and Benjamin of all the "abominable idols" in the land.

For forty-one years Asa reigned in Jerusalem. He was one of the best kings Judah ever had. He made some mistakes, of course, but his heart was "perfect with the Lord all his days." And that's a wonderful thing for God to say about anybody

STORY 8

From Bad to Worse

IN THE northern kingdom of Israel things were going from bad to worse. After Jeroboam died his son Nadab took the throne. But he was as bad as his father, and "did evil in the sight of the Lord."

Nadab didn't last long—barely two years. Then a man named Baasha rebelled against him, killed him, and took his throne.

To make sure that no other son of Jeroboam's would try to take the kingdom away from him, Baasha "smote all the house of Jeroboam; he left not . . . any that breathed," just as Ahijah the prophet had said would happen.

Baasha reigned twenty-four years, but he wasn't any better than Jeroboam. "He did evil in the sight of the Lord," even though God did send the prophet Jehu to warn him of what would happen to him if he refused to mend his ways.

When Baasha died his son Elah came to the throne and reigned two years. He was a drunkard, and Zimri, captain

190

of half the king's chariots, conspired against him and slew him.

Zimri made himself king, but held the throne only seven days, during which time he killed all the relatives of Baasha. While he was busy doing this, the people of Israel made Omri king.

Omri and his men marched on the capital city of Tirzah, where Zimri was living, and captured it. "And when Zimri saw that the city was taken, . . . he went into the palace of the king's house, and burnt the king's house over him with fire, and died."

That was the end of Zimri, but Omri's troubles were not over yet. Another man named Tibni rose up and drew half the people after him. So there was more fighting until "Tibni died, and Omri reigned."

Omri was king twelve years. During his reign he did one thing of great importance. He bought a hill for two talents of silver and built a city on it. He called this city Samaria, and moved his capital there.

It was a great chance to start all over again. Everything was new and clean and beautiful. All that was evil, all that belonged to the bad old days, could have been left behind. Yet while two talents of silver could buy a hill, they could not make it holy. They could buy houses and lands, and maybe a new palace for the king, but not peace and righteousness. Something more was needed for that, and nobody had it.

When Omri died, Ahab his son reigned in his stead. "And it came to pass, as if it had been a light thing for him to walk in the sins of Jeroboam the son of Nebat, that he took to wife Jezebel the daughter of Eth-baal king of the Zidonians, and went and served Baal, and worshipped him. And he reared up an altar for Baal in the house of Baal, which he had built in Samaria. . . . And Ahab did more to provoke the Lord God of Israel to anger than all the kings of Israel that were before him."

Thus, fifty years after the death of Solomon, the people of Israel had completely turned their backs on God. Their king was an idolater, their queen a heathen, and their capital city boasted a temple to Baal. Things could not have been much worse. The stage was set for the coming of Elijah the prophet.